Slice of Success:

A Recipe for Turning Your Struggling Pizzeria into a Thriving Business

By Mark Lowe

Pizzeria Wellness Index

Instructions: This assessment is designed to measure the overall wellness of a pizzeria based on the topics covered in this workbook. For each statement, select the response that best reflects the current state of your pizzeria. The scoring key and interpretation are provided at the end of the assessment.

Scoring: 0 = Strongly Disagree 1 = Disagree 2 = Somewhat Disagree 3 = Somewhat Agree 4 = Agree 5 = Strongly Agree

1. We have a clear mission statement that guides our business decisions. 0 1 2 3 4 5

2. We have a well-defined target market and understand their needs and preferences. 0 1 2 3 4 5

3. We have a solid financial management system that includes budgeting and forecasting. 0 1 2 3 4 5

4. We use cost control strategies to minimize expenses without sacrificing quality. 0 1 2 3 4 5

5. We incorporate sustainable practices in our operations. 0 1 2 3 4 5

6. We actively engage with our local community and support local causes. 0 1 2 3 4 5

7. We have a strong online presence and utilize digital marketing strategies. 0 1 2 3 4 5

8. We have a solid employee management system that includes training, development, and retention. 0 1 2 3 4 5

9. We regularly gather feedback from customers and use it to improve our business. 0 1 2 3 4 5

10. We have a system in place for measuring and evaluating the success of our business strategies. 0 1 2 3 4 5

Scoring Key: 45-50: Excellent - Your pizzeria is performing exceptionally well in all areas. 35-44: Good - Your pizzeria is doing well, but there is room for improvement in some areas. 25-34: Fair - Your pizzeria could benefit from significant improvements in several areas. 0-24: Poor - Your pizzeria needs immediate attention and significant improvements in multiple areas.

Interpretation: This assessment provides a comprehensive evaluation of the overall wellness of a pizzeria. By measuring key factors such as mission statement, target market, financial management, cost control, sustainable practices, community engagement, online presence, employee management, customer feedback, and strategy evaluation, pizzeria owners can gain insight into areas where they are performing well and areas where they need to improve.

This workbook provides a wealth of information and resources on each of these topics, along with practical tips and strategies for implementing them. By working through the exercises and implementing the strategies outlined in this workbook, pizzeria owners can improve the overall wellness of their business and set themselves up for success.

In six months, after working through the book and implementing new strategies, retake the Pizzeria Index, then again six months after that to compare and track your progress.

Chapter 1: Introduction

Welcome to "Slice of Success: A Recipe for Turning Your Struggling Pizzeria into a Thriving Business." Owning and operating a pizzeria can be challenging, with stiff competition, high costs, and demanding customers. But with the right approach and strategies, your pizzeria can become a successful and profitable business.

This workbook is designed to help struggling pizzeria owners navigate these challenges and achieve their goals. It provides practical advice and step-by-step guidance to help you assess your current state, develop a business plan, build your brand, improve operations, and more.

Through a combination of exercises, templates, and case studies, you will learn how to identify your target market, create a marketing strategy, design an effective menu, improve customer service, and manage your finances. You will also learn how to utilize technology, online platforms, and social media to enhance your online presence and attract new customers.

Whether you are just starting out or looking to revitalize your existing pizzeria, this workbook offers the tools and insights you need to succeed. By following the strategies outlined in this workbook, you will be able to take your pizzeria to the next level, increase profits, and create a loyal customer base.

To use this book effectively, you can follow these steps:

1. Read through each chapter carefully and take notes on the key points and strategies discussed.

2. Implement the strategies learned in each chapter in your pizzeria. Take the time to evaluate which strategies are most applicable to your business and prioritize those.

3. Monitor your progress and track the impact of each strategy on your pizzeria's success. Use the assessment provided at the end of the book to gauge the overall wellness of your pizzeria.

4. Seek additional resources and support as needed. This can include consulting with industry experts, attending workshops or seminars, or seeking advice from other successful pizzeria owners.

By following these steps and using the strategies presented in this book, you can improve the overall success and wellness of your pizzeria.

So, let's get started on your journey to success!

PizzaRev, a fast-casual pizza chain with locations throughout the United States. Despite having a popular concept and attracting initial investor interest, the chain faced financial difficulties due to high operating costs and stiff competition in the crowded fast-casual pizza market.

In 2019, PizzaRev filed for Chapter 11 bankruptcy protection and closed several underperforming locations. The chain also underwent a leadership change, with a new CEO taking over and implementing changes to improve profitability. This included streamlining operations, simplifying the menu, and investing in technology to improve customer experience and increase efficiency.

Despite these efforts, PizzaRev still faces challenges in a highly competitive market, with many consumers turning to delivery and takeout options during the COVID-19 pandemic. The chain continues to explore new strategies to stay relevant and profitable, such as partnering with third-party delivery services and expanding their menu offerings.

Following the bankruptcy filing and leadership change, PizzaRev implemented several changes to improve its financial position. This included closing underperforming locations, negotiating more favorable lease agreements, and implementing cost-saving measures.

In addition to these operational changes, PizzaRev also sought to improve its menu offerings and customer experience. The chain introduced new menu items, such as gluten-free and cauliflower crust options, and invested in technology to streamline the ordering and payment process.

Despite these efforts, the COVID-19 pandemic had a significant impact on the restaurant industry, and PizzaRev was no exception. The chain was forced to close several locations temporarily and pivot to takeout and delivery-only models. However, PizzaRev was able to adapt quickly to these challenges, leveraging its existing technology and partnerships with third-party delivery services to continue serving customers during the pandemic.

As of 2021, PizzaRev continues to operate over 30 locations throughout the United States, with a focus on expanding its presence in key markets. The chain has also continued to innovate, introducing new menu items and partnerships with popular brands to attract customers. While PizzaRev still faces challenges in a crowded market, the chain's ability to adapt and innovate gives hope for its continued success in the future.

Why is it so hard to run a pizzeria?

Running a pizzeria can be a challenging endeavor due to various factors. Firstly, competition in the restaurant industry is fierce, and pizzerias must find ways to differentiate themselves from others. This could be by creating a unique style or signature pizza or offering exceptional customer service to stand out in the crowded market.

Secondly, costs can be a significant challenge, including the expenses of ingredients, equipment, and labor. Pizzerias must maintain high-quality ingredients, but this can be costly, especially if they aim to use fresh, organic produce. Additionally, labor costs can be high, especially if the pizzeria is in an area with a high minimum wage.

Thirdly, customers have high expectations when it comes to pizza. They want hot, fresh, and delicious pizzas delivered quickly, and they expect excellent customer service whether they're dining in or ordering delivery. To meet these expectations, pizzerias must have skilled staff who can produce high-quality pizzas consistently.

Finally, running a pizzeria is time-consuming and requires effort. Owners must manage inventory, schedules, and staff, while also dealing with unexpected challenges like equipment malfunctions or customer complaints. It can be a demanding job that requires long hours and a hands-on approach.

Despite these challenges, owning and operating a pizzeria can be incredibly rewarding. A successful pizzeria can bring a sense of community, joy, and profitability to its owners and customers. By understanding and overcoming the challenges, pizzeria owners can achieve their goals and create a thriving business.

This workbook is designed to help pizzeria owners overcome the challenges they face and achieve their business goals. The workbook offers practical advice and strategies for addressing key challenges, such as competition, costs, customer expectations, and time management.

Chapter by chapter, the workbook covers a range of topics relevant to pizzeria owners, such as branding and marketing, menu development, cost management, customer service, and employee management. Each chapter includes actionable tips and exercises designed to help pizzeria owners implement the strategies discussed and improve their business operations.

Additionally, the workbook includes case studies and success stories from successful pizzeria owners who have overcome similar challenges. By learning from these real-world examples, readers can gain insights into what works and what doesn't in the pizzeria business.

Overall, Slice of Success is an invaluable resource for any pizzeria owner looking to improve their business operations and achieve success in a competitive market. By implementing the strategies and tips discussed in the workbook, pizzeria owners can take their business to the next level and build a loyal customer base that will support their success over the long term.

1. What are some common challenges faced by pizzeria owners?

2. How do factors like location, competition, and changing consumer preferences impact the success of a pizzeria?

3. In what ways can staffing, inventory management, and equipment maintenance pose challenges for pizzeria owners?

4. How does financial planning play a role in overcoming the challenges of running a pizzeria?

Chapter 2:

Assessing Your Pizzeria's Current State

"You can't improve what you don't measure." - Peter Drucker

This chapter is all about assessing your pizzeria's current state. Before you can develop strategies to improve your business, it's essential to understand where you stand now. This chapter is designed to help you take a step back and evaluate your pizzeria's strengths, weaknesses, opportunities, and threats.

The chapter begins by discussing why a current state assessment is essential for pizzeria owners. It explains that an honest evaluation of your business can help you identify areas for improvement, prioritize your efforts, and ultimately achieve your goals. It also explains that the assessment process can help you make data-driven decisions and avoid costly mistakes.

The chapter then delves into the various elements of a current state assessment. It covers topics such as evaluating your menu, analyzing your competition, understanding your customer base, and assessing your finances. Each section includes detailed guidance on how to approach the assessment and what questions to ask yourself.

Throughout the chapter, readers are encouraged to take notes and complete exercises that will help them identify areas of strength and weakness in their business. By the end of the chapter, readers should have a clear understanding of where their pizzeria stands and what areas they need to focus on to achieve their goals.

Overall, this chapter is an essential resource for any pizzeria owner looking to improve their business operations. By taking the time to assess their current state and identify areas for improvement, pizzeria owners can lay the groundwork for success and take their business to the next level.

Evaluating your business performance

How might evaluating your business help? Let's say A small, family-owned pizzeria in a suburban area of California had been experiencing a decrease in sales and customer traffic for several months. The owners were puzzled because they had a loyal customer base and always received positive feedback about their food and service.

To try and figure out what was going on, they decided to evaluate their business performance. They started by analyzing their sales data and found that their lunchtime sales had decreased by almost 30% compared to the previous year.

They then began to look at other factors that could be contributing to the decline in sales, such as changes in the local economy, competition from other pizzerias, and changes in customer preferences.

They discovered that a new fast-food restaurant had recently opened nearby, which was attracting a lot of customers during the lunch hours. The pizzeria owners also noticed that many of their regular customers were looking for healthier and more diverse options for lunch, which they were not currently offering.

Armed with this information, the owners decided to make changes to their menu, including adding more salads, wraps, and vegetarian options. They also started a new lunchtime promotion that offered discounted prices for customers who ordered in advance.

As a result of these changes, their lunchtime sales started to pick up, and they were able to attract new customers who were looking for healthier and more diverse options. By evaluating their business performance and making changes based on the data, the pizzeria was able to turn around their declining sales and stay competitive in their market.

Evaluating your business performance is a critical step in understanding how well your pizzeria is performing and identifying areas where you can make improvements. There are several key metrics that you should regularly track and analyze to get an accurate picture of your business performance, including sales data, customer feedback, and employee performance.

Sales data is one of the most important metrics to track when evaluating your business performance. By analyzing your sales data, you can identify trends in customer behavior, such as peak hours and popular menu items. You can also track changes in revenue over time to identify potential problems or opportunities for growth.

Another key metric to evaluate is customer feedback. Gathering feedback from your customers can help you understand their preferences and identify areas where you can improve your food quality, customer service, or overall experience. This feedback can be collected through surveys, online reviews, or direct feedback from customers who visit your pizzeria.

Employee performance is also an important metric to evaluate when assessing your business performance. Your employees play a critical role in providing excellent customer service and ensuring that your pizzeria operates smoothly. By monitoring employee performance, you can identify areas where additional training or support may be needed to help them perform their jobs more effectively.

Once you have evaluated your business performance, you can use the data you have gathered to make informed decisions about how to improve your pizzeria. For example, if your sales data shows that certain menu items are not selling as well as others, you can consider revising your menu to offer more popular items or adjusting prices to better reflect customer demand. Similarly, if customer feedback indicates that your staff needs additional training or support, you can invest in training programs to help them improve their skills and provide better service.

Overall, evaluating your business performance is essential for achieving long-term success as a pizzeria owner. By regularly tracking and analyzing key metrics, you can identify areas for improvement, make informed decisions about your business, and stay competitive in your market.

1. Why is it important to evaluate your business regularly?

2. What are some key performance indicators to consider when evaluating your business?

3. How can evaluating your business help you identify areas for improvement?

4. What are some common challenges businesses face when evaluating their performance?

Identifying strengths and weaknesses

To run a successful pizzeria, it's essential to have a clear understanding of your business's strengths and weaknesses. This involves taking a close look at every aspect of your business, from your menu and pricing strategy to your marketing efforts and customer service. By identifying your strengths and weaknesses, you can make informed decisions about how to allocate resources, prioritize initiatives, and make improvements to help your business succeed.

One effective way to identify your business's strengths and weaknesses is to conduct a SWOT analysis. SWOT stands for strengths, weaknesses, opportunities, and threats. This analysis involves evaluating your business's internal strengths and weaknesses, as well as external opportunities and threats in the market. By doing so, you can gain a comprehensive understanding of your business's current state, as well as the potential opportunities and challenges that lie ahead.

To conduct a SWOT analysis, start by brainstorming a list of your pizzeria's strengths and weaknesses. This might include things like the quality of your food, the expertise of your staff, your pricing strategy, your marketing efforts, or your location. Once you have a list of strengths and weaknesses, you can move on to identifying opportunities and threats in the market. This might involve researching industry trends, evaluating the competitive landscape, or analyzing customer behavior.

Ultimately, the goal of identifying your strengths and weaknesses is to gain a clear understanding of your business's current state and potential for growth. By conducting a SWOT analysis, you can make informed decisions about where to focus your efforts, prioritize initiatives, and make improvements to help your business succeed over the long term.

Determining your pizzeria's strengths and weaknesses requires a comprehensive evaluation of your business from every angle. This means taking a close look at every aspect of your operations, from your menu and pricing strategy to your marketing efforts and customer service.

To identify your pizzeria's strengths, start by considering what sets your business apart from your competitors. This might include things like the quality of your food, the expertise of your staff, the ambiance of your restaurant, or the convenience of your location. You might also look to customer feedback and reviews to identify areas where your business excels.

On the other hand, identifying weaknesses requires a critical assessment of areas where your business falls short or could improve. This might include things like menu items that don't sell well, inefficiencies in your operations, or areas where your customer service could be improved. You might also look to customer feedback and reviews to identify common complaints or issues that customers experience.

It's important to approach the process of identifying strengths and weaknesses with an open mind and a willingness to acknowledge areas where improvements can be made. This can be challenging, but it's an essential part of running a successful pizzeria. Once you've identified your strengths and weaknesses, you can develop strategies to build on your strengths and address weaknesses to help your business grow and succeed.

Here are some key questions to consider:

1. How are sales trending over time, and are there any patterns or trends in customer behavior that you can identify?

2. Are there any menu items that are not selling well, and should they be replaced or adjusted to improve sales?

3. How does your pricing compare to that of your competitors, and are there opportunities to adjust your pricing strategy to better reflect customer demand?

4. What do your customers say about their experience at your pizzeria, and are there any common complaints or concerns that you should address?

5. How well do your employees perform, and are there any areas where additional training or support is needed to improve their skills?

6. Are there any operational inefficiencies that are costing you time or money, and how can you address them?

7. How does your online presence compare to that of your competitors, and are there opportunities to improve your website, social media, or other digital marketing efforts?

8. What are the latest industry trends, and are there any opportunities to capitalize on them to grow your business?

By asking these and other questions, you can gain a more complete picture of your pizzeria's business performance, identify areas for improvement, and make informed decisions to help your business succeed over the long term.

Analyzing competition

Analyzing the competition is an important part of running a successful pizzeria. By evaluating your competitors, you can gain a better understanding of the market, identify opportunities to differentiate your business, and develop strategies to attract and retain customers.

Analyzing your competition involves evaluating their strengths and weaknesses, pricing strategies, menu offerings, customer service, marketing efforts, and any other factors that may impact their success. This information can be used to identify areas where you can differentiate your business and offer a unique value proposition to customers.

Let's say you. own a small pizzeria that specializes in New York-style pizza. To analyze the competition, you might start by researching other pizzerias in your area that offer similar types of pizza.

After visiting their websites, social media pages, and reading customer reviews, you may find that one of your main competitors offers a wider variety of toppings and has a more extensive menu overall. Another competitor may have a more modern, trendy aesthetic that appeals to younger customers.

You could also visit these competitor pizzerias in person to evaluate factors like the quality of the food, the friendliness of the staff, the cleanliness of the restaurant, and the overall customer experience. You might also consider factors like pricing strategies and marketing efforts to evaluate how these competitors position themselves in the market.

Once you've completed your analysis, you can use this information to identify opportunities to differentiate your business from the competition. For example, you may decide to focus on offering high-quality, authentic New York-style pizza with fewer, but more carefully selected toppings. Alternatively, you might decide to improve your customer service or invest in marketing efforts to build brand awareness and attract new customers.

By taking a thoughtful approach to analyzing the competition, you can gain a better understanding of the market and develop strategies to position your pizzeria for success over the long term.

While it's important to be aware of your competition, it's also important to remember that your pizzeria's success ultimately depends on your ability to offer a high-quality product, exceptional customer service, and a unique value proposition to customers. By analyzing the competition and identifying areas for improvement, you can make informed decisions about how to position your business in the market and build a loyal customer base over time.

1. Who are the top competitors in your local market, and what are their strengths and weaknesses?

2. How does your business differentiate itself from the competition?

3. What strategies do your competitors use to attract and retain customers?

4. How can you leverage the knowledge gained from analyzing your competition to improve your business strategy?

Chapter 3:

Developing a Business Plan, Again

"Your business plan is not a one-time document, but a living roadmap that evolves with your pizzeria's journey."

Developing a business plan is a crucial step in starting and running a successful pizzeria. A business plan serves as a roadmap for your business, outlining your goals, strategies, and tactics for achieving success over the long term.

However, it's important to note that developing a business plan is not a one-time task. As your business evolves and the market changes, it's important to revisit and update your business plan to ensure that it remains relevant and effective.

Revisiting your business plan allows you to assess your progress, adjust your strategies, and make any necessary changes to ensure that you are on track to achieving your goals. It also provides an opportunity to reassess your market, evaluate new opportunities, and refine your value proposition to stay competitive in a constantly evolving industry.

In this chapter, we will discuss the key components of a comprehensive business plan, including your mission statement, market analysis, marketing strategies, financial projections, and more. We'll also explore best practices for updating and revising your business plan to ensure that it remains an effective tool for guiding your business toward success over the long term.

In an interview with CNBC, Elon Musk, CEO of Tesla and SpaceX emphasized the importance of having a clear and comprehensive business plan, stating that "a business plan is really a plan for how you're going to solve a problem."

Musk went on to explain that a business plan should not just be a document to secure funding, but rather a living roadmap that guides the direction of the business over the long term. He emphasized the importance of regularly revisiting and updating the plan as the market evolves and ensuring that the plan remains relevant and effective.

Musk's success as a visionary entrepreneur and business leader serves as a testament to the value of having a strong and adaptable business plan. By developing a comprehensive plan and regularly revisiting it, business owners can stay focused on their goals and adapt to changing market conditions, ultimately leading to greater success over the long term.

Below is a basic outline of a business plan. All you need to do is fill out the missing information.

1. Executive Summary

- Brief overview of the pizzeria business, mission statement, and goals

2. Company Description

- Background information on the pizzeria, including history and location

- Description of the products and services offered

3. Market Analysis

- Analysis of the local market and competition

- Identification of target market and customer demographics

4. Marketing and Sales Strategy

- Plan for advertising, promotions, and public relations

- Sales strategy, including pricing, discounts, and loyalty programs

5. Menu and Service

- Detailed menu and pricing strategy

- Overview of the restaurant service and operations, including delivery options

6. Management and Staffing

- Description of the management team and key personnel

- Staffing plan and personnel requirements

7. Financial Plan

- Overview of start-up and operating costs

- Financial projections, including revenue, expenses, and profits

- Funding strategy and sources of capital

Let's talk about some areas where you should pay extra attention when writing your plan.

Market analysis is the process of researching and evaluating the local market and competition to understand the current and potential demand for your products or services. It is an important step in developing a business plan, as it can help you identify opportunities and challenges, and inform your marketing and sales strategy.

To conduct a market analysis for a pizzeria, you should start by researching the local market and competition. This may include:

1. Identifying other pizzerias in the area, including their location, menu, pricing, and reputation.

2. Understanding the size and demographics of the local population, including income levels, age groups, and family size.

3. Examining trends in the local restaurant industry, such as changes in customer preferences or new market entrants.

4. Conducting surveys or focus groups with potential customers to gather feedback on your product offerings and pricing.

Once you have gathered this information, you can use it to identify your target market and customer demographics. This may include:

1. Defining your ideal customer profile, including their age, income, location, and other characteristics.

2. Developing marketing and sales strategies that target this ideal customer profile.

3. Identifying opportunities to differentiate your pizzeria from competitors, such as by offering unique menu items or delivery options.

Here are some questions to answer.

Who is my target customer and what are their demographics?

How does my competition target their customers and what strategies can I use to differentiate myself?

What are the current market trends in the pizza industry and how can I take advantage of them?

What are the strengths and weaknesses of my location and how can I leverage them in my marketing strategy?

Your Ideal Customer

Defining your ideal customer profile is an important step in developing a successful business strategy for your pizzeria. Here are some steps to help you define your ideal customer profile:

Start by researching your local market and competition to understand who your potential customers are. Look at the demographics of your local area, including age, income, and lifestyle, and consider how these factors may influence their pizza-buying behavior.

Use customer data from your existing customer base if you have one. This may include information on their demographics, preferences, and behavior.

Develop a customer persona that represents your ideal customer. This persona should be a fictional representation of your ideal customer, based on your research and customer data. Consider factors such as age, income, location, family size, and lifestyle, as well as their pizza preferences and purchasing behavior.

Refine your customer persona by testing it against your target market. Conduct surveys or focus groups to gather feedback on your customer persona and ensure that it accurately represents your target market.

Use your customer persona to inform your marketing and sales strategies. Tailor your messaging, promotions, and product offerings to appeal to your ideal customer, and use data analytics to track their behavior and preferences over time.

1. What are the demographic characteristics of my ideal customer?

2. What are the interests and behaviors of my target audience?

3. How can I tailor my marketing messages to better resonate with my ideal customer?

4. Are there any common pain points or challenges that my target audience is facing that my product or service can address?

Overall, defining your ideal customer profile is a key step in developing a successful business strategy for your pizzeria. By understanding who your customers are and what motivates them, you can tailor your offerings to meet their needs and build a loyal customer base.

Creating a marketing strategy

In a 2019 interview with Forbes, Shama Hyder, CEO of Zen Media, emphasized the importance of creating a strong marketing strategy for businesses.

She stated, "Your marketing strategy is your North Star. It's what keeps you focused and ensures that your marketing efforts are aligned with your overall business goals. Without a marketing strategy, you're throwing things against the wall and hoping something sticks."

Hyder advised businesses to research their target audience, define their unique value proposition, and develop a content strategy to effectively communicate with their audience.

She also emphasized the importance of regularly tracking and analyzing the success of marketing efforts to make informed adjustments and improvements.

Creating a marketing strategy for your pizzeria is essential to attract and retain customers. A marketing strategy involves a set of tactics and activities designed to promote your business, increase awareness, and drive sales. Here are some steps to help you create an effective marketing strategy for your pizzeria:

1. Define your target market: Start by identifying your ideal customer profile, including their demographics, behavior, and preferences. This will help you tailor your marketing efforts to your target audience.

2. Conduct a competitive analysis: Research your competitors to understand their marketing strategies, messaging, and promotions. This will help you differentiate your business and identify areas of opportunity.

3. Define your unique selling proposition (USP): Determine what sets your pizzeria apart from the competition and use this as the foundation for your marketing messaging.

4. Develop a marketing mix: Determine which marketing tactics will be most effective for your business, such as social media, email marketing, local advertising, and promotions.

5. Set marketing goals and metrics: Establish measurable goals for your marketing efforts, such as increasing website traffic, improving customer retention, or increasing sales. Use data analytics to track your progress and adjust your marketing strategy as needed.

6. Create a marketing budget: Determine how much you can afford to spend on marketing activities and allocate your budget based on the tactics that will have the most impact.

7. Implement and measure your marketing strategy: Launch your marketing activities and track their effectiveness using data

analytics. Adjust your strategy as needed to improve results and achieve your goals.

Here is an example of how a marketing strategy my look. Mama's Pizzeria wanted to attract more families with children, so they developed a marketing strategy that focused on promoting their family-friendly atmosphere and kid-friendly menu options. They created a special "Family Fun Night" promotion every Wednesday, where families could get a large pizza, a pitcher of soda, and a side of garlic knots for a discounted price. They also added a "Create Your Own Pizza" option for kids, where they could choose their own toppings and watch their pizza being made in the kitchen.

To promote this new strategy, Mama's Pizzeria updated their website with new photos and descriptions of their family-friendly offerings, and they posted about it on their social media channels. They also created a flyer that they distributed in local neighborhoods, and they put up posters in the restaurant to promote the new promotion. Finally, they partnered with a local family-friendly event and set up a booth to give out free pizza samples and coupons for their Family Fun Night promotion.

As a result of their marketing strategy, Mama's Pizzeria saw an increase in families with children coming in on Wednesdays, and they also received positive feedback from customers about the new kid-friendly options.

Creating a marketing strategy is a critical component of building a successful pizzeria business. By understanding your target market, differentiating your business, and implementing effective marketing tactics, you can attract and retain customers, increase sales, and grow your business over time.

1. What is your target audience and how will you reach them?

2. What unique selling proposition does your pizzeria have and how will it be communicated to potential customers?

3. How will you measure the success of your marketing efforts?

4. How will you adjust your marketing strategy over time to account for changes in the market or customer preferences?

Setting goals and objectives

"Setting goals is the first step in turning the invisible into the visible." - Tony Robbins

Tony Robbins, a renowned business and life coach, emphasizes the importance of setting goals and objectives for personal and professional growth. He believes that setting clear and achievable goals can help individuals and businesses move forward and achieve success.

Robbins advises breaking down long-term goals into smaller, more manageable objectives to ensure progress is being made. By regularly reviewing and adjusting these goals and objectives, businesses can stay focused and motivated to achieve their desired outcomes.

Robbins also stresses the importance of setting measurable goals and objectives that are specific, realistic, and relevant to the business's overall mission and vision. By doing so, businesses can track their progress and make necessary adjustments to their strategies to achieve their goals.

Overall, Tony Robbins highlights the importance of setting goals and objectives as a foundational step towards achieving success in business and life.

Setting goals and objectives is an essential part of running a successful pizzeria. These goals help you to focus your efforts and make progress towards your desired outcome. Setting clear and specific goals and objectives can help you to measure your success and stay motivated as you work towards achieving them.

When setting goals, it is important to consider both short-term and long-term objectives. Short-term goals should be achievable within a relatively short time frame, such as a few months, while long-term goals may take several years to accomplish.

To set effective goals, start by identifying what you want to achieve. This could include increasing revenue, expanding your customer base, or improving your restaurant's reputation. Once you have identified your goals, break them down into smaller, more manageable tasks that you can work on each day or week.

It is also important to make your goals specific and measurable. For example, instead of setting a goal to "increase sales," set a specific target such as "increase sales by 10% in the next six months." This allows you to measure your progress and adjust your strategy if necessary.

Additionally, setting realistic goals is crucial to your success. While it is important to aim high, setting goals that are too lofty can be demotivating if they are not achieved. Consider your current resources, market conditions, and other factors when setting your goals.

Here are some additional examples you may want to set for your business.

Here are some examples:

1. Increase sales by 15% in the next six months through a combination of marketing campaigns, special promotions, and improved customer service.

2. Improve customer satisfaction by maintaining a 4.5-star rating or higher on popular review sites like Yelp and Google.

3. Expand the business by opening a second location in a nearby town within the next two years.

4. Reduce overhead costs by 10% in the next year through a combination of energy-efficient equipment upgrades and tighter budgeting.

5. Increase online ordering by 25% in the next six months by improving the online ordering process and promoting the convenience of ordering through the restaurant's website and mobile app.

6. Expand the menu by introducing healthier options, such as gluten-free crusts and vegan toppings, to attract a wider range of customers.

7. Increase employee retention by implementing a training and development program that provides opportunities for career growth and advancement within the company.

8. Increase community involvement by sponsoring local events and participating in charity drives to build a positive reputation and strengthen relationships with customers and other businesses in the area.

9. Improve the restaurant's environmental sustainability by reducing waste and implementing recycling programs.

10. Improve profitability by maintaining a consistent profit margin of at least 15% through regular financial monitoring and analysis.

Finally, it is important to regularly review and adjust your goals as needed. This allows you to stay on track and make necessary changes if your strategy is not working. By setting clear goals and objectives, you can focus your efforts, measure your success, and achieve long-term success for your pizzeria.

1. What are the specific, measurable goals that I want my pizzeria to achieve in the next year?

2. How can I ensure that my goals align with my pizzeria's overall mission and values?

3. What strategies can I implement to achieve my goals within the given time frame?

4. How will I track and measure the success of my goals, and what adjustments will I make if necessary?

Financial Planning

financial planning is essential for developing a successful business plan. It involves identifying all potential sources of revenue, such as sales and investments, and assessing expenses, such as overhead costs and salaries. Financial planning allows business owners to make informed decisions about how to allocate resources and make investments that can help the business grow and succeed.

By developing a comprehensive financial plan, pizzeria owners can set realistic financial goals for their business and ensure they have the resources to achieve them. This includes forecasting sales and expenses, setting budgets, and tracking cash flow to ensure the business remains financially stable. Additionally, financial planning helps identify potential challenges and risks, allowing owners to develop contingency plans to mitigate them.

Financial planning also plays a crucial role in securing financing and attracting investors. By presenting a clear and comprehensive financial plan, business owners can demonstrate to lenders and investors that they have a solid understanding of the financial aspects of their business and a plan to achieve their goals.

Here's an example of financial planning you may want to consider.

A pizzeria owner wants to expand their business by opening a new location. They start by creating a financial plan that includes projections for revenue, expenses, and profits. They research the cost of leasing a new space, hiring additional staff, and purchasing equipment and inventory.

Based on their projections, they determine that they will need to secure a loan to cover the upfront costs of opening the new location. They create a detailed budget that considers all the expenses they will incur, from rent and utilities to marketing and insurance.

They also set financial goals for the new location, such as achieving a certain level of revenue and profitability within the first year. They regularly review their financial statements and adjust their plan as needed to ensure they stay on track to meet their goals.

Through careful financial planning, the pizzeria owner can successfully open the new location and grow their business.

1. What are the key financial metrics that should be tracked in a pizzeria, and how often should they be reviewed?

2. How can a pizzeria balance its expenses and revenue to maximize profitability?

3. What strategies can be employed to manage cash flow effectively in a pizzeria?

4. What are some potential risks to the financial health of a pizzeria, and how can they be mitigated through proper planning and management?

Overall, financial planning is a critical component of developing a successful business plan for pizzeria owners. It allows them to make informed decisions about their business, set achievable financial goals, and ensure the financial stability of their business.

1. Define your financial goals and objectives.

2. Conduct a financial analysis of your pizzeria, including revenue, expenses, and cash flow.

3. Create a budget for your pizzeria based on your financial analysis and goals.

4. Develop strategies to increase revenue and decrease expenses.

5. Monitor and review your financial plan regularly to track progress and make necessary adjustments.

Chapter 4

Building Your Brand

"A strong brand is not just a logo or a name, it's an experience that customers remember and trust."

In today's competitive business landscape, branding has become more important than ever before. Your brand is the unique identity that your business creates, it distinguishes your business from competitors and helps customers to remember and trust your business. Building a brand for your pizzeria is an essential component of your overall marketing strategy. It creates the foundation of your business identity and communicates your values, beliefs, and vision to your target audience.

Building your brand is not just about creating a name or logo for your business; it is about building a unique and memorable identity that resonates with your customers. It is an ongoing process that requires consistent effort, focus, and creativity. In this chapter, we will discuss the various elements of building a strong brand for your pizzeria, including brand strategy, brand identity, brand voice, and brand messaging.

A strong brand can help your pizzeria stand out in a crowded market and attract loyal customers. It creates a positive perception of your business and helps customers to remember your brand. A well-crafted brand strategy can also help you to align your business goals with your customer's needs and expectations.

In the following sections, we will discuss the key elements of building a strong brand for your pizzeria, provide examples of successful pizzeria branding, and offer practical tips for creating a unique and memorable brand identity for your business. Whether you are just starting or looking to refresh your existing brand, this chapter will help you to build a solid foundation for your brand and take your business to the next level.

Creating a unique identity for your pizzeria

Paulie Gee's in Brooklyn, New York, started as a small pizzeria with a unique concept – they only offered Neapolitan-style pizza with creative and unusual toppings. They also had a rustic, hipster vibe, with a focus on quality ingredients and handcrafted pizzas. Paulie Gee's was successful in creating a cult following of customers who appreciated their creative approach and high-quality food. Today, Paulie Gee's has expanded to multiple locations in Brooklyn, Chicago, Columbus, and Baltimore, but they have maintained their unique identity and commitment to quality, creative pizzas.

Creating a unique identity for your pizzeria is an essential part of building a successful brand that stands out from the competition. Your pizzeria's identity should communicate what makes your business special and what customers can expect from their experience with your brand.

The first step in creating a unique identity for your pizzeria is to understand your target audience. Who are your customers? What do they want from their dining experience? What makes your pizza unique, and how can you communicate this to your audience? These are important questions to consider as you start to build your brand.

Once you have a clear understanding of your target audience and what sets your pizza apart, it's time to start thinking about your visual identity. This includes your logo, color scheme, typography, and any other visual elements that will be associated with your brand.

Your logo is the centerpiece of your visual identity and should reflect the unique personality and values of your pizzeria. It's important to invest in a professional logo design that will resonate with your target audience and communicate the essence of your brand.

Your color scheme should be consistent with your brand's personality and values. For example, if your pizzeria is all about fun and excitement, you may want to use bright, bold colors. If you want to communicate a more sophisticated and elegant vibe, you may want to use muted, understated colors.

Typography is also an important aspect of your visual identity. The font you choose should be legible and easy to read, but it should also reflect your brand's personality. For example, if your pizzeria is all about fun and excitement, you may want to use a playful and whimsical font. If you want to communicate sophistication and elegance, you may want to use a more classic and traditional font.

In addition to your visual identity, your pizzeria's unique identity should also be reflected in your marketing and advertising campaigns. This includes everything from your website and social media presence to your print and radio ads.

Your messaging should be consistent with your brand's values and personality. If you're all about fun and excitement, your messaging should reflect this. If you want to communicate a more sophisticated and elegant vibe, your messaging should be refined and sophisticated as well.

It's also important to make sure your advertising campaigns are targeted to your specific audience. For example, if you're targeting families with children, you may want to run ads on family-friendly websites and in parenting magazines.

Finally, your pizzeria's unique identity should be reflected in every aspect of your business. This includes everything from the design of your restaurant to the way your employees interact with customers.

When customers walk into your restaurant, they should immediately get a sense of your pizzeria's personality and values. Your employees should be trained to communicate this personality and value to customers, whether it's through their interactions or through the food and drinks they serve.

Here is an example to consider. John, a young entrepreneur, has always dreamed of opening his own pizzeria. He knows the competition is fierce in his town, with at least five well-established pizzerias within a two-mile radius. However, John believes he can offer something unique and exciting that will set his pizzeria apart from the others.

First, John conducts thorough market research to better understand his target customers and the competition. He analyzes the demographics of the area, the types of pizza that are popular, and the prices charged by his competitors. Through this research, he identifies a gap in the market for affordable, high-quality pizza that is made with fresh and locally sourced ingredients.

Next, John creates a customer persona, or a fictional representation of his ideal customer. He imagines his ideal customer is a young professional in their mid-twenties who values quality ingredients and is willing to pay a little more for a great pizza. John gives this persona a name, "Healthy Holly," and uses her preferences and characteristics to guide his menu development and marketing strategies.

With his target customer and unique selling proposition in mind, John sets out to create a brand identity that will attract and resonate with his target market. He hires a graphic designer to create a logo that incorporates a fresh and modern aesthetic, with bold colors and imagery of locally grown produce. He also invests in a custom website and social media accounts that showcase his commitment to quality ingredients and sustainability.

To further differentiate his pizzeria, John offers a unique menu with innovative toppings and flavor combinations that appeal to his target customer. He also offers gluten-free and vegan options to cater to a wider range of dietary needs and preferences.

Finally, John focuses on creating a memorable customer experience that sets his pizzeria apart from the competition. He trains his staff to be knowledgeable about the menu and ingredients, and to provide friendly and attentive service. He also offers an inviting atmosphere with comfortable seating, ambient lighting, and local art on the walls.

Through these efforts, John can successfully create a unique identity for his pizzeria that sets it apart from the competition and attracts his target customer. He sees a steady stream of loyal customers and positive reviews, and his pizzeria becomes a beloved fixture in the local community.

1. What values do you want your pizzeria to embody and how can you communicate them through branding?

2. How can you differentiate your pizzeria from competitors in the area?

3. Have you considered the demographics and preferences of your target market in crafting your brand identity?

4. Are you willing to invest the time and resources necessary to create a strong and consistent brand identity for your pizzeria?

In conclusion, creating a unique identity for your pizzeria is essential to building a successful brand that stands out from the competition. It requires a deep understanding of your target audience, a cohesive visual identity, consistent messaging, and a commitment to embodying your brand's values in every aspect of your business. By investing time and resources into developing a unique identity, you can create a brand that customers will love and that will set your pizzeria apart from the rest.

Developing a brand strategy

Developing a brand strategy refers to the process of creating a plan to establish and promote a unique brand identity for a business. It involves defining the brand's core values, personality, target audience, and visual elements, such as the logo, color scheme, and typography.

An example of a brand strategy is Apple's "Think Different" campaign. Apple's brand strategy focused on positioning the company as a leader in innovation and creativity. They used the "Think Different" slogan to appeal to consumers who wanted to stand out and be different from the norm. The brand's visual elements, such as the sleek and minimalist design of their products and the iconic Apple logo, also contributed to their overall brand identity.

To develop a brand strategy, businesses should consider their target audience, competitors, and unique selling points. It is important to have a clear understanding of what sets the brand apart from competitors and how it can be effectively communicated to the target audience. This may involve conducting market research, analyzing competitors' brand strategies, and identifying the brand's unique strengths and values.

Another important aspect of developing a brand strategy is consistency. Once the brand's identity has been established, it is important to ensure that it is consistently reflected in all aspects of the business, from marketing materials to customer service interactions. This helps to build trust and recognition among consumers and reinforces the brand's overall message and values.

Overall, developing a brand strategy is an essential part of establishing a strong and memorable brand identity. By taking the time to define the brand's core values and personality, businesses can create a unique identity that resonates with their target audience and helps to differentiate them from competitors.

Here is an example of how a strategy may look.

Brand Purpose: To provide high-quality, delicious pizza to our customers while creating a warm, welcoming atmosphere where friends and family can gather and enjoy their time together.

Brand Values: Quality - We use only the freshest, high-quality ingredients in all of our pizzas. Community - We value our community and seek to create a warm, welcoming atmosphere in our pizzeria. Authenticity - Our pizzas are made with authentic recipes and cooking techniques, inspired by our Italian heritage. Innovation - We are constantly experimenting with new flavors and toppings to keep our menu fresh and exciting.

Target Audience: Our target audience is families and young adults aged 18-35 who are looking for a fun and relaxed dining experience with friends and family.

Brand Personality: Our brand personality is warm, inviting, and authentic. We want our customers to feel like they are stepping into a cozy Italian kitchen where they can relax and enjoy their time together.

Brand Positioning: Our pizzeria is positioned as the go-to spot for high-quality, authentic pizza in a warm and welcoming atmosphere. We offer a diverse menu of classic and innovative pizzas, as well as a variety of sides and drinks to create a well-rounded dining experience.

Brand Promise: We promise to provide our customers with the highest quality, most delicious pizzas possible, while creating a warm, welcoming environment that feels like home. We are dedicated to constantly improving and innovating to keep our menu fresh and exciting.

1. What makes my brand unique compared to competitors in the market?

2. How can I effectively communicate my brand's values and message to potential customers?

3. Is my brand strategy aligned with the target audience and their preferences?

4. How can I measure the success of my brand strategy and adjust as needed?

Designing a logo and signage

Designing a logo and signage is the process of creating a visual representation of your brand through a unique and recognizable logo, as well as signage that reflects your brand identity and attracts customers to your business.

An example of designing a logo and signage for a pizzeria would involve creating a logo that incorporates pizza imagery, such as a slice of pizza or a chef tossing dough, and using warm and inviting colors like red, orange, and yellow to evoke feelings of comfort and coziness. The signage should be easily visible and legible from a distance, with clear fonts and easy-to-read text.

Here are four questions to consider when designing a logo and signage for your pizzeria:

1. What message do you want to convey with your logo and signage?

2. What colors and imagery best reflect your brand identity and values?

3. How can you make your logo and signage stand out from other pizzerias in the area?

4. How can you ensure that your logo and signage are easily recognizable and memorable for customers?

Make your logo compelling and memorable. Think about The Nike "swoosh" logo is a well-known example of an effective and iconic logo design. The logo was designed in 1971 by graphic designer Carolyn Davidson, who was a student at Portland State University at the time.

Nike co-founder Phil Knight had met Davidson while she was working on a project for a class and asked her to design a logo for his new athletic shoe company.

Davidson created several designs, but Knight ultimately chose the simple "swoosh" design, which he felt represented the motion and speed of athletics. The logo has since become synonymous with the Nike brand and is instantly recognizable around the world.

Implementing consistent branding across all channels

Implementing consistent branding across all channels involves maintaining a unified brand identity and messaging across all customer touchpoints, including website, social media, advertising, packaging, and customer service. Consistency in branding helps customers identify and differentiate your brand from competitors, increases brand awareness, and fosters brand loyalty.

For example, Coca-Cola's branding consistently features its iconic red and white colors, unique font, and distinct logo across all advertising channels, product packaging, and promotional materials. The brand's messaging also consistently promotes happiness, positivity, and refreshment, reinforcing its image as a trusted, iconic brand in the beverage industry.

Implementing consistent branding also involves regularly monitoring and evaluating the effectiveness of branding efforts across all channels, identifying areas for improvement, and making necessary adjustments to maintain consistency and relevance in the ever-evolving marketplace.

Implementing consistent branding across all channels involves ensuring that your brand identity is maintained and reinforced in all communication and marketing efforts. This can be done by following a set of guidelines and standards for how your brand should be presented.

Here are some steps to implementing consistent branding:

1. Develop a style guide: This should include guidelines for logo usage, color schemes, typography, imagery, and tone of voice. It should be a comprehensive document that outlines all of the visual and messaging components of your brand.

2. Train employees: Make sure all employees understand the importance of consistent branding and how to use the style guide. Provide training on how to use logos, fonts, and colors correctly, and how to write and speak in the brand's voice.

3. Use consistent visuals: Ensure that all visuals used across all channels, including social media, website, print materials, and advertising, adhere to the brand's style guide. This means using the same colors, fonts, and imagery.

4. Use consistent messaging: Make sure that all messaging is consistent across all channels. This includes using the same tone of voice and key messaging points in all marketing materials.

5. Monitor and adjust: Regularly review and analyze all channels to ensure that branding is consistent and effective. Adjust as needed to improve brand messaging and visual identity.

In conclusion, building a strong brand identity for your pizzeria is crucial for attracting and retaining customers. It involves creating a unique brand strategy, designing a distinctive logo and signage, and implementing consistent branding across all channels. By doing so, you can establish a strong emotional connection with your target audience, build brand recognition, and differentiate your pizzeria from competitors.

Here are four questions for reflection on building your brand:

What makes your pizzeria unique and how can you incorporate that into your brand strategy?

How can you design a logo and signage that accurately reflects your brand personality and values?

In what ways can you ensure consistent branding across all channels, including your website, social media, and physical storefront?

How can you measure the effectiveness of your branding efforts and adjust as needed to better resonate with your target audience?

Chapter 5:

Menu Development

"Your menu is not just a list of dishes, it's a story about your brand, your values, and your passion for food."

Understanding your customers' preferences is a crucial aspect of menu creation for any restaurant, including a pizzeria. By identifying the tastes and preferences of your target market, you can create a menu that appeals to their preferences and drives repeat business.

One of the best ways to understand your customers' preferences is by conducting market research. This can include online surveys, focus groups, or simply observing customer behavior and feedback. You can use this data to determine which types of pizza toppings, sauces, and crust styles are most popular among your customer base.

Here are some example questions you can ask.

Sure, here are some examples of focus group and survey questions that could be used to understand customers' preferences for a pizzeria menu:

Focus Group Questions:

1. What kind of pizza toppings do you prefer?

2. Do you prefer traditional toppings or more unconventional ones?

3. What are some of your favorite pizza flavors?

4. What would make you more likely to order pizza from a specific pizzeria?

5. Are there any specific dietary restrictions or preferences that should be taken into account for menu items?

Survey Questions:

1. How often do you order pizza from a restaurant?

2. What is your favorite type of crust for pizza?

3. Do you prefer classic pizza toppings or more unique ones?

4. Would you be interested in a build-your-own-pizza option?

5. On a scale of 1-10, how important is the quality of ingredients when ordering pizza?

These questions can help gather valuable insights about customers' pizza preferences, which can be used to inform menu creation and overall business strategy.

Another important factor to consider is dietary restrictions and preferences. In today's health-conscious environment, many customers are looking for options that fit their specific dietary needs, such as gluten-free crusts or vegetarian toppings. Offering a variety of options that cater to these preferences can help broaden your customer base and increase sales.

It's also important to stay on top of industry trends and seasonal changes in food preferences. For example, incorporating seasonal toppings or limited time offers can generate excitement and drive sales. Similarly, keeping up with popular trends in the pizza industry, such as Detroit-style or Neapolitan-style pizza, can help set your pizzeria apart from competitors.

Overall, understanding your customers' preferences is an ongoing process that requires attention to detail and a willingness to adapt. By staying in tune with your customers and regularly updating your menu, you can create a satisfying dining experience that keeps customers coming back for more.

4 questions for reflection:

1. What methods have you used to understand your customers' preferences?

2. How can you incorporate dietary restrictions and preferences into your menu?

3. How can you stay on top of industry trends and incorporate them into your menu?

4. In what ways can you continue to adapt and update your menu to better suit your customers' preferences?

Designing a menu that reflects your brand and target market

Once upon a time, there was a small Italian restaurant that had been in business for many years. The owner, Marco, was proud of his restaurant's authentic Italian cuisine and family-friendly atmosphere. However, he noticed that his restaurant was not attracting as many customers as it used to, and he was struggling to keep up with the competition.

One day, Marco decided to revamp his menu to better reflect his brand and target market. He wanted to create a menu that would appeal to both new and loyal customers. He started by conducting surveys and focus groups to better understand his customers' preferences.

The surveys asked customers about their favorite Italian dishes, how often they dined out, and what factors influenced their restaurant choices. The focus groups were more in-depth, with participants tasting new menu items and providing feedback on the flavors, presentation, and pricing.

Armed with this information, Marco worked with his chefs to create a new menu that incorporated classic Italian dishes with a modern twist. He added more vegetarian and gluten-free options to cater to the growing number of customers with dietary restrictions. He also revamped the restaurant's decor to better reflect the new menu and create a more inviting atmosphere.

The changes were an instant success. Customers raved about the new menu items, and the restaurant's social media presence grew as diners shared photos of their meals online. Marco was thrilled to see his restaurant once again thriving and attracting new customers. He knew that understanding his customers' preferences and designing a menu that reflected his brand and target market were key to his success.

A well-designed menu can showcase your unique offerings, highlight your brand values, and ultimately, help attract and retain customers.

For example, if your pizzeria caters to health-conscious customers, you may want to include a variety of salads and vegetarian options on your menu. On the other hand, if your target market is families with young children, you may want to offer a range of kid-friendly options and family meal deals.

To design a menu that reflects your brand and target market, you should consider factors such as:

1. Brand values and identity: Think about how your menu can showcase your unique brand values and identity. For example, if your brand is all about quality, you may want to highlight the premium ingredients you use.

2. Target market preferences: Conduct market research to understand your target market's preferences and what they're looking for in a menu. This information can help you tailor your offerings to meet their needs.

3. Menu layout and design: Consider the layout and design of your menu, including the placement of items, the use of images and descriptions, and the overall look and feel.

4. Pricing strategy: Determine your pricing strategy and ensure your menu reflects it. For example, if you're targeting budget-conscious customers, you may want to offer more affordable options or value deals.

Example menu items that reflect your brand and target market could include:

- For a health-conscious target market: Kale salad, gluten-free pizza crust, vegan cheese options, and low-carb cauliflower crust pizza.

- For a target market of families with young children: Kid-sized pizzas, family meal deals, and dessert options like cookie dough or brownies.

Overall, designing a menu that reflects your brand and target market requires careful consideration of your customers' preferences, market research, and branding elements.

Here are some reflection questions.

1. How well do you understand your target market and their preferences when it comes to food choices?

2. In what ways does your menu reflect your brand and appeal to your target market?

3. Have you conducted focus groups or surveys to gather feedback on your menu? If not, how could you integrate this into your menu design process?

4. How often do you review and update your menu to keep up with changing customer preferences and food trends?

Pricing Strategy

Pricing strategies are essential in determining the value of your products and services, while also influencing customer behavior. Effective pricing strategies ensure profitability, while also ensuring your products are accessible to your target market.

One popular pricing strategy is cost-plus pricing, where you calculate the cost of production and add a markup to determine the selling price. Another strategy is value-based pricing, which focuses on the perceived value of your product or service to the customer. In this approach, you set prices based on the benefits the product or service provides to the customer, as opposed to the cost of production.

Dynamic pricing is another popular pricing strategy. This involves changing the price of your product or service in real-time based on factors such as supply and demand, time of day, and even the weather.

Psychological pricing is also worth considering. This involves setting prices to influence customers' perception of value, such as pricing products just below a round number (e.g., $4.99 instead of $5.00) or highlighting a discount (e.g., $10 off).

Here are some examples and best practices for each pricing strategy:

1. Cost-plus pricing: This involves adding a markup to the cost of producing a product to determine the final selling price.

Here is an example of how to determine the cost of a pizza. Add up the cost of ingredients including box, napkins, utensils, cups, lids, and bag-- everything. Next, figure the time to make it multiply by employee wages for that time. Then figure the cost of your lease, utilities, insurance, advertising, etc. Then figure your other expenses and taxes. After figuring the true cost of your item then you can add your mark up. I have an easier way. Food costs should be 20% + Wages 25% + fixed costs of 20% + other expenses 20% = 85%. This leaves 15% for profit. So, take your food cost and multiply by 5 or 6 and that will give you a sustainable retail price.

2. Dynamic pricing: This involves adjusting prices in real-time based on factors such as demand, time of day, or seasonality. For example, a pizzeria may offer lower prices during slow periods to attract customers and raise prices during peak hours when demand is high.

Best practices for dynamic pricing include regularly analyzing sales data to identify patterns and adjust pricing accordingly. It's also important to clearly communicate to customers when prices may fluctuate, and to avoid pricing too high during peak periods as it may deter customers.

3. Psychological pricing: This involves using pricing techniques that appeal to customers' emotions or perceptions, rather than strictly based on the cost of production or market demand. For example, pricing an item at $9.99 instead of $10 can make it seem more affordable to customers.

Best practices for psychological pricing include testing different pricing strategies to see what resonates with customers, as well as considering the brand image and target market when deciding on pricing techniques. It's also important to be transparent with customers and avoid using deceptive pricing tactics that may erode trust.

When deciding on a pricing strategy, it is important to consider your target market, competitors, and industry norms. Conducting market research and testing different pricing strategies can help you determine the most effective pricing strategy for your business.

In summary, pricing strategies are a critical aspect of running a successful business. The right pricing strategy can help increase profitability, attract customers, and create a perception of value for your products or services.

Here are some questions to reflect on when considering pricing strategies:

1. What is my target market, and how do they perceive value?

2. What are my competitors charging for similar products or services, and how can I differentiate my pricing strategy?

3. What are the production costs for my products or services, and how can I ensure profitability while remaining competitive?

4. How can I adjust my pricing strategy in response to changes in demand or industry trends?

Menu Engineering

Menu engineering is the process of analyzing a restaurant's menu to maximize profitability and sales. It involves analyzing the popularity and profitability of each menu item to determine the best way to price and promote them. The goal of menu engineering is to increase revenue by strategically positioning menu items and adjusting prices to appeal to customers and drive profits.

To start, menu engineering involves categorizing menu items into four categories: stars, plow horses, puzzles, and dogs. Stars are high-profit and high-popularity items, while plow horses are high-popularity but low-profit items. Puzzles are low-popularity but high-profit items, and dogs are low-popularity and low-profit items.

Once menu items have been categorized, pricing strategies and promotion efforts can be adjusted accordingly. For example, stars can be priced higher since they are popular and profitable, while plow horses can be promoted more heavily to increase their profitability. Puzzles may require additional marketing efforts to increase their popularity, while dogs may need to be removed from the menu altogether.

Menu engineering also involves analyzing the cost of ingredients and labor for each menu item to determine the most profitable pricing strategy. Cost-plus pricing involves calculating the cost of ingredients and labor and adding a markup to determine the final price. Dynamic pricing adjusts prices based on demand and other market factors, while psychological pricing utilizes pricing strategies that appeal to customers' emotions and perception of value.

Overall, menu engineering is a critical aspect of restaurant management as it helps maximize profitability and sales by strategically pricing and promoting menu items.

1. What pricing strategies have you used in the past for your business? Were they successful? Why or why not?

2. Have you ever conducted focus groups or surveys to understand your customers' preferences? If not, how do you plan to gather this information in the future?

3. How important do you think menu engineering is to the success of a restaurant? Have you ever analyzed your menu in this way? If so, what changes did you make based on your analysis?

4. How does your menu reflect your brand and target market? Is there anything you could do to improve this alignment?

Chapter 6:

Operational Excellence

"Consistent execution is the foundation of operational excellence."

In 1993, a small coffee shop called Starbucks opened its doors in the Pike Place Market in Seattle. At that time, the coffee industry was saturated with big players like Folgers and Maxwell House, and independent shops had to work hard to differentiate themselves. However, Starbucks had a vision to offer something different - a unique experience centered around quality coffee and a welcoming atmosphere.

Starbucks quickly became known for its focus on operational excellence, from the way they sourced and roasted their coffee to the consistency of their drinks and the atmosphere of their stores. This focus on operational excellence allowed them to scale their business rapidly, and today there are over 32,000 Starbucks locations worldwide. Their success has inspired countless other businesses to prioritize operational excellence in their own operations, making it a critical element of any successful business strategy.

Operational excellence is the art of running your business in a way that maximizes efficiency, productivity, and customer satisfaction. At its core, it's about optimizing every aspect of your operations to deliver high-quality products and services to your customers while minimizing costs and waste. This can be achieved through a variety of practices such as continuous improvement, process optimization, and technology integration. In this chapter, we'll explore the key principles of operational excellence and how they can be applied to your pizzeria to enhance performance, reduce waste, and increase profitability.

Streamlining Operations

Streamlining operations is the process of optimizing and improving the efficiency of a business's operational processes to increase productivity, reduce waste, and save time and resources. It involves analyzing the current processes, identifying areas of improvement, and implementing changes to eliminate bottlenecks and improve overall efficiency.

In the restaurant industry, streamlining operations is crucial to running a successful and profitable business. From the kitchen to the front of the house, there are a variety of operational processes that must run smoothly to provide a positive experience for customers and maximize profits.

There are several strategies that can be used to streamline operations in a restaurant, such as implementing a point-of-sale system to track orders and inventory, optimizing the kitchen layout to improve workflow, and cross-training employees to handle multiple tasks.

By streamlining operations, restaurants can reduce costs, improve the quality of service, and increase customer satisfaction, ultimately leading to a more successful and profitable business.

Let's say in your own pizzeria and have noticed that your kitchen staff is frequently running into each other as they try to move around the kitchen and prepare orders. You've also noticed that customers are occasionally waiting longer than they should for their orders to be ready. You decide to streamline your operations to improve efficiency and customer satisfaction.

First, you rearrange the layout of your kitchen to create more space for your staff to move around without getting in each other's way. You also purchase additional kitchen equipment, such as a second oven and a larger prep table, to help speed up the cooking process.

Next, you implement a system for taking and preparing orders that reduces the risk of miscommunication and speeds up the process. For example, you might have one staff member designated to take orders and another to prepare them, with a clear system for tracking which orders have been placed and which are ready to go.

You also work with your staff to create clear standard operating procedures (SOPs) for each task, from taking orders to preparing dough to cleaning the kitchen. This helps ensure consistency and efficiency in your operations.

Overall, your efforts to streamline your operations have paid off. Your staff can work more efficiently, resulting in faster order times and happier customers. You've also reduced the risk of errors or miscommunication, leading to greater consistency in the quality of your food and service.

Here are some reflection questions.

1. What are the areas of your business that can benefit from streamlining operations, and how can you achieve this?

2. What are the potential benefits and drawbacks of implementing operational efficiencies, such as automation or outsourcing?

3. How can you maintain a focus on quality and customer satisfaction while streamlining operations?

4. What metrics can you use to measure the success of operational improvements, and how can you continually optimize your processes?

Developing Efficient Processes

As the owner of a small pizzeria, you're always looking for ways to improve your operations and make things run more smoothly. One day, you decided to take a closer look at your ordering process and realized that it was taking longer than it needed to. Customers were often waiting in line for several minutes just to place their orders, and some even left without ordering because they didn't want to wait.

You knew you had to do something to speed things up, so you started to brainstorm ways to streamline the process. After some careful consideration, you decided to install a self-serve kiosk where customers could place their orders themselves. You also added a mobile ordering option so that customers could place their orders from their phones and pick them up when they arrived.

To ensure that customers knew about these new options, you updated your menu and signage to promote them. You even sent out an email to your customer list letting them know about the changes and encouraging them to try out the new self-serve kiosk and mobile ordering options.

The results were almost immediate. Customers were now able to place their orders much more quickly, and the lines moved much faster. You also noticed an increase in mobile orders, which helped to further streamline the process and reduce wait times for customers.

Overall, you were thrilled with the results of your efforts to streamline your ordering process. By taking a close look at your operations and making some simple changes, you were able to greatly improve the customer experience and make your pizzeria more efficient and profitable.

Developing efficient processes involves the identification and improvement of existing workflows and procedures to optimize the use of resources and reduce waste. By streamlining operations, businesses can save time, reduce costs, and improve overall productivity. Continuing these processes requires a deep understanding of the business's operations and can involve the use of various tools such as process mapping, automation, and technology.

Businesses should start by analyzing existing workflows to identify inefficiencies and areas for improvement. This can involve working with employees at all levels of the organization to gain a comprehensive understanding of current processes and identify bottlenecks or areas where manual processes could be automated.

Once inefficiencies have been identified, businesses can develop and implement strategies to streamline operations. This may involve introducing new technology or automation tools, reorganizing the workforce to improve communication and collaboration, or making changes to the physical layout of the workplace.

Developing efficient processes is an ongoing process that requires continuous evaluation and improvement. By regularly monitoring operations and adjusting as necessary, businesses can optimize their processes and stay competitive in an ever-changing market.

Some best practices for developing efficient processes include involving employees at all levels in the process, using data to inform decision-making, regularly reviewing, and updating processes, and implementing technology and automation where appropriate.

Examples of efficient processes might include automating inventory management, implementing a paperless system for invoicing and billing, or creating a standardized process for onboarding new employees.

Overall, developing efficient processes is essential for any business looking to improve productivity, reduce costs, and stay competitive in the marketplace.

Some reflection questions for businesses looking to develop efficient processes might include:

1. What are the current inefficiencies in our operations?

2. How can we involve employees in the process of developing more efficient workflows?

3. What technology or automation tools could we implement to streamline operations?

4. How can we regularly review and update our processes to ensure continued efficiency?

Hiring and training staff

"Train people well enough so they can leave, treat them well enough so they don't want to." - Richard Branson

Hiring and training staff is a critical aspect of achieving operational excellence in any business, including a pizzeria. Your employees are the face of your business, and they can make or break the customer experience. Therefore, it is essential to hire the right people, train them effectively, and provide ongoing support to ensure they are performing at their best.

When it comes to hiring staff, it's crucial to have a clear idea of the roles and responsibilities you need to fill. This means developing job descriptions and job ads that accurately reflect the requirements of the position. Once you have a pool of candidates, it's essential to conduct thorough interviews to ensure that they have the right skills, experience, and personality traits that fit with your business.

When hiring new staff, it is important to prioritize personality traits that align with the company's culture and values. A friendly, outgoing personality with a passion for customer service can go a long way in creating a positive experience for customers. Additionally, hiring individuals with a strong work ethic, attention to detail, and the ability to work well in a team can lead to a more efficient and productive workplace.

Here are some best practices for hiring:

1. Look for people who are passionate about food: When hiring staff, it's important to look for individuals who are passionate about food and the restaurant industry. This passion will translate into excellent customer service and a commitment to quality.

2. Prioritize reliability: Pizzerias often operate on tight schedules, so it's important to prioritize reliability when hiring staff. Look for individuals who have a track record of showing up on time and completing tasks on schedule.

3. Conduct thorough interviews: Take the time to conduct thorough interviews with each candidate, asking questions that will help you determine if they are a good fit for the job. In addition to discussing their experience and skills, ask questions about their work ethic, personality, and availability.

4. Provide comprehensive training: Once you have hired staff, it's important to provide them with comprehensive training to ensure they can perform their duties to the best of their abilities. This includes training on how to make pizzas, customer service, and handling cash and credit card transactions.

5. Foster a positive work environment: Finally, it's important to foster a positive work environment at your pizzeria. This includes treating employees with respect, providing opportunities for professional growth, and offering incentives for hard work and exceptional performance. Happy employees are more likely to provide excellent customer service and contribute to the success of your business.

Training is another critical component of developing an effective team. New hires need to receive comprehensive training that covers everything from the menu and the ordering system to food safety and customer service. Ongoing training is also essential to ensure that your team is always up to date with the latest industry trends, customer preferences, and best practices.

An employee handbook is a valuable tool in the training process of new hires. It provides an overview of the company's policies and procedures, as well as outlines the expectations for behavior and job performance. This helps new hires understand their role within the company and how to fulfill their job duties.

In addition to an employee handbook, outside training can also be beneficial for pizzeria staff. For example, a training program focused on customer service can improve the overall experience for customers, leading to increased customer loyalty and repeat business. Additionally, training on proper food handling and safety practices can ensure that the pizzeria is operating in compliance with health and safety regulations.

Here is an outline of an employee manual you may want to use.

An employee handbook is an essential document that outlines the policies, procedures, and expectations of the company for its employees. Here is an outline of what should be included in an employee handbook:

1. Introduction: Introduce the company and its mission statement, as well as the purpose and importance of the employee handbook.

2. Employment policies: Explain the company's employment policies, including equal opportunity, anti-discrimination, harassment, and retaliation policies. Include policies on employment eligibility, job classifications, and employee benefits.

3. Code of conduct: Describe the company's code of conduct and ethical standards. This section should outline expected employee behavior, dress code, attendance policy, and standards for punctuality.

4. Safety and security: Explain the company's safety and security policies, including emergency procedures, workplace safety rules, and protocols for reporting accidents or injuries.

5. Compensation and benefits: Detail the company's pay and benefits packages, including employee compensation, time off policies, vacation and sick leave, and other fringe benefits.

6. Performance expectations: Provide guidelines on performance expectations, such as job duties, evaluation criteria, and goals.

7. Training and development: Outline the company's training and development programs, including orientation and onboarding, career development opportunities, and performance improvement plans.

8. Employee grievances: Describe the process for addressing employee grievances, including how to report concerns or complaints, and what actions the company will take to resolve issues.

9. Acknowledgment and signature: Provide space for the employee to acknowledge that they have received and read the employee handbook and sign off on their understanding of the contents.

An employee handbook is an important tool for training and guiding employees. In addition to creating an employee handbook, outside training and professional development opportunities can help employees to develop new skills and increase productivity. Providing training opportunities can also help employees feel valued and invested in the company's success.

In terms of training, on-the-job training should be provided to new hires to ensure they are equipped with the necessary skills to perform their job duties. This can include training on how to properly prepare and cook pizza, how to handle customer inquiries and complaints, and how to use the point-of-sale system.

Investing in your employees can yield significant returns. When employees feel valued and supported, they are more likely to be motivated, engaged, and committed to their work. This can translate into higher job satisfaction, lower staff turnover rates, and ultimately, a better customer experience.

In summary, hiring and training staff are critical components of achieving operational excellence in a pizzeria. By hiring the right people, training them effectively, and providing ongoing support, you can build a strong team that delivers exceptional customer experiences and helps your business thrive.

1. What steps can I take to improve my hiring process and ensure that I am attracting and selecting the best candidates for my pizzeria?

2. How can I provide ongoing training and development opportunities for my staff to ensure that they are equipped with the skills and knowledge necessary to excel in their roles?

3. What policies and procedures should be included in my pizzeria's employee handbook to ensure that my employees are informed and equipped to perform their jobs effectively?

4. How can I foster a positive and supportive work environment that encourages teamwork, collaboration, and a commitment to operational excellence among my staff?

Implementing technology to improve operations

In recent years, Domino's has invested heavily in technology to streamline its operations and improve the customer experience. Some of the ways they have done this include:

1. Online Ordering: Domino's was one of the first pizza chains to offer online ordering. Customers can place an order through the company's website or mobile app, which saves time and reduces errors.

2. GPS Tracking: To improve delivery times and reduce the number of wrong orders, Domino's uses GPS tracking to monitor the progress of its delivery drivers in real-time.

3. Automated Pizza-Making: Domino's has also experimented with automated pizza-making machines. These machines can make pizzas faster and more consistently than human workers.

4. Virtual Assistant: In 2017, Domino's introduced a virtual assistant called "Dom" that can take orders via text message, Facebook Messenger, and other platforms. This makes it easier for customers to order pizza without having to call the restaurant.

By implementing these and other technologies, Domino's has been able to improve its operations, reduce costs, and provide a better customer experience.

Implementing technology in a business can significantly improve operations, streamline processes, and enhance the overall customer experience. In today's fast-paced world, customers expect quick and efficient service, and technology can help businesses meet those expectations.

One area where technology can be implemented is in the ordering process. A pizzeria can implement online ordering through a website or mobile app, allowing customers to place orders at their convenience. This can reduce the wait time for customers, and the orders can be processed more quickly and accurately, reducing the chances of errors.

Another area where technology can be useful is in inventory management. Implementing a point-of-sale (POS) system can help track inventory levels, alerting the business when certain items are running low. This can help businesses avoid running out of key ingredients during peak hours, ensuring they can continue to meet customer demands.

Including an app for ordering is a great way to streamline operations and improve the customer experience at your pizzeria. With an app, customers can easily place their order from the comfort of their own device, without the need for a phone call or in-person visit. This can help to reduce wait times and increase order accuracy, as customers can take their time to review their order and make any necessary changes before submitting it.

When implementing an app for ordering, it's important to choose a platform that is user-friendly and reliable. There are many app development companies that specialize in creating customized ordering apps for restaurants, so it's worth doing some research to find one that fits your needs and budget. Some popular options include Toast, Grubhub, and Square.

In addition to an ordering app, there are many other types of technology that can help improve operations at your pizzeria. For example, using a point-of-sale (POS) system can help to streamline transactions and track inventory. Online ordering platforms and delivery management systems can also be helpful for managing orders and deliveries.

It's important to keep in mind that implementing new technology can be a significant investment, both in terms of time and money. It's important to carefully weigh the costs and benefits before making any decisions. Additionally, it's important to provide adequate training and support to your staff to ensure they are comfortable and proficient in using the new technology.

Overall, implementing technology to improve operations can be a great way to enhance the customer experience and increase efficiency at your pizzeria. By taking the time to carefully research and choose the right tools, and providing sufficient training and support, you can set your business up for success in the increasingly digital world of food service.

Some resources for implementing technology in a pizzeria include:

- Restaurant Technology Network (https://restauranttechnologynetwork.com/)

- National Restaurant Association (https://restaurant.org/)

- Pizza Today (https://www.pizzatoday.com/)

Technology can also be used for employee scheduling and timekeeping. Implementing software that allows employees to clock in and out electronically can help eliminate errors and reduce the time spent on payroll processing. Additionally, scheduling software can help managers schedule employees more efficiently, reducing the chances of being over or understaffed during busy periods.

Lastly, technology can be used for marketing purposes, such as email marketing campaigns, social media management, and customer relationship management (CRM) systems. These tools can help businesses build and maintain relationships with their customers, keeping them informed about promotions, new menu items, and other news.

While implementing technology can have many benefits, it's important to remember that it's not a substitute for human interaction. Businesses should ensure that they maintain a balance between technology and personal interactions, providing excellent customer service while also leveraging technology to improve operations.

In summary, implementing technology can greatly improve a pizzeria's operations, from ordering and inventory management to employee scheduling and marketing. By embracing technology and finding the right tools for their needs, businesses can enhance the customer experience and increase efficiency.

Questions for reflection:

1. What are the benefits and drawbacks of implementing technology in a business?

2. How can technology be used to improve operations in my own business?

3. What steps should be taken to ensure a smooth transition when implementing new technology?

4. How can customer feedback be used to improve the technology and overall operations of the business?

Chapter 7:

Customer Service

"The customer may not always be right, but they should always feel valued and heard."

Zappos, an online shoe, and clothing retailer, is known for its "WOW" customer service, which emphasizes going above and beyond to satisfy customers.

For example, Zappos offers free shipping both ways, so customers can return items for any reason without any additional cost. They also have a 365-day return policy, which is much longer than most other retailers. In addition, Zappos has a team of customer service representatives available 24/7 to answer questions and resolve any issues.

Zappos also focuses on creating a positive company culture, which they believe translates into better customer service. They offer employees benefits such as free food and on-site wellness programs and encourage them to personalize their interactions with customers.

Overall, Zappos' commitment to exceptional customer service has helped to set them apart in a competitive online retail market.

Exceptional customer service can lead to loyal customers, positive reviews, and increased profitability. In this chapter, we will discuss various strategies that can help improve customer service, including the importance of building relationships with customers, training employees, and handling customer complaints effectively.

By providing a memorable customer experience, pizzeria businesses can stand out in a competitive market and build a strong reputation that drives repeat business.

Understanding the importance of excellent customer service

Understanding the importance of excellent customer service is essential for any business, including a pizzeria. Customers expect to be treated with respect and professionalism, and their experience can make or break a business. Excellent customer service can lead to repeat business and positive word-of-mouth advertising, while poor customer service can result in negative reviews and a loss of customers.

Providing excellent customer service can involve various elements, including prompt and friendly service, personalized attention, and addressing any issues or concerns that arise. It also involves creating a welcoming and inviting atmosphere, where customers feel comfortable and valued.

As a pizzeria owner, it's important to train your staff to provide excellent customer service, from the way they answer the phone to how they handle customer complaints. It's also important to listen to customer feedback and use it to improve the customer experience.

Ultimately, the goal of excellent customer service is to create a positive and memorable experience for your customers, leading to loyalty and positive word-of-mouth recommendations.

Customer service is the act of providing assistance and support to customers before, during, and after their purchase. It is an integral part of any business, but it is especially important in the restaurant industry. Customers not only expect quality food but also a pleasant atmosphere and outstanding service.

Excellent customer service can lead to increased customer loyalty, positive word-of-mouth advertising, and ultimately increased revenue. Conversely, poor customer service can lead to negative reviews, decreased customer loyalty, and decreased revenue.

Providing excellent customer service starts with understanding the needs and wants of your customers. By doing so, you can tailor your service to their expectations and improve their overall experience. There are various ways to understand your customers' needs, such as customer surveys, social media feedback, and online reviews.

Customer Surveys

Customer surveys can provide valuable insight into what your customers think of your restaurant and the service you provide. Surveys can be conducted in person or online, and they can cover various topics such as food quality, atmosphere, and service. By asking customers to rate their experience and provide feedback, you can identify areas for improvement and make the necessary changes.

Social Media Feedback

Social media is a powerful tool for businesses to engage with their customers and receive feedback. Many customers use social media platforms to share their experiences with friends and family, and by monitoring these platforms, you can gain insight into how your restaurant is perceived. Responding to customer feedback, whether positive or negative, shows that you care about your customers and are committed to improving their experience.

Online Reviews

Online reviews, such as those on Yelp or Google, can provide valuable feedback on your restaurant's service and overall experience. By monitoring these reviews and responding to them, you can show that you are listening to your customers and are committed to providing excellent service.

After gathering feedback from customers, it's important to analyze and take action on the insights gained. For example, if customers consistently complain about long wait times for their food, the restaurant can work on improving kitchen efficiency or hiring additional staff to address the issue. On the other hand, if customers provide positive feedback about a specific aspect of the restaurant, such as friendly staff or a particular menu item, the restaurant can continue to emphasize and promote those strengths.

Additionally, responding to feedback can show customers that their opinions are valued and can help to build loyalty. If a customer leaves a negative review online, responding with a thoughtful and empathetic message can show that the restaurant is willing to listen and improve. On the other hand, thanking customers for positive feedback can help to reinforce their positive experience and encourage them to return.

Ultimately, acting on customer feedback is crucial for improving the overall customer experience and ensuring long-term success for the business.

Here is an example of a customer feedback survey for social media:

1. How likely are you to recommend our pizzeria to a friend or family member on social media?

- Very likely

- Likely

- Neutral

- Unlikely

- Very unlikely

2. On a scale of 1-10, how satisfied were you with your recent experience at our pizzeria?

- 1 (not satisfied at all)

- 2

- 3

- 4

- 5 (neutral)

- 6

- 7

- 8

- 9

- 10 (very satisfied)

3. What did you enjoy most about your experience at our pizzeria?

- Food quality

- Speed of service

- Cleanliness of the restaurant

- Friendliness of the staff

- Atmosphere and ambiance

- Other (please specify)

4. What could we have done to make your experience better?

- Lower prices

- Better food quality

- Faster service

- Cleaner restaurant

- Friendlier staff

- Better atmosphere and ambiance

- Other (please specify)

5. Would you be willing to provide a review of our pizzeria on social media?

- Yes

- No

- Maybe

6. Do you follow our pizzeria on social media?

- Yes

- No

7. If you answered "no" to question 6, would you be willing to follow us on social media?

- Yes

- No

- Maybe

8. Is there anything else you would like to share about your experience at our pizzeria?

Here are some reflection questions.

1. How do you currently handle customer feedback in your business?

2. What are some potential benefits and drawbacks of implementing a customer feedback survey through social media?

3. How can you use customer feedback to improve your business operations and customer service?

4. In what ways can you go above and beyond to exceed customer expectations and provide exceptional service?

Developing a customer service strategy

Ritz-Carlton is a luxury hotel chain that is renowned for its exceptional customer service. The company's customer service strategy is centered around their "Gold Standards", which outline the key behaviors and actions that their employees should consistently exhibit to provide outstanding service.

One example of the Gold Standards in action is the "Anticipation and Fulfillment" standard. This means that Ritz-Carlton employees should anticipate the needs and preferences of guests before they even ask, and go above and beyond to fulfill those needs in a personalized and thoughtful way.

For instance, if a guest is staying at the hotel for a special occasion like a birthday or anniversary, Ritz-Carlton employees may arrange for a surprise gift or amenity to be delivered to their room. Or, if a guest mentions a preference for a certain type of pillow or bedding, the hotel staff will make sure that those preferences are noted and accommodated for future stays.

In addition to the Gold Standards, Ritz-Carlton also places a strong emphasis on employee training and empowerment. The company invests heavily in employee training and development to ensure that their staff has the skills, knowledge, and resources needed to provide exceptional service. Additionally, Ritz-Carlton empowers their employees to make decisions and take actions that will enhance the guest experience, giving them the flexibility to go above and beyond to delight customers.

Overall, Ritz-Carlton's customer service strategy is characterized by a relentless focus on the customer, a commitment to excellence, and a culture of empowerment and continuous improvement.

Developing a customer service strategy is an essential aspect of any successful business. It involves identifying the target market and developing a plan to ensure customer satisfaction through all stages of the customer journey. This can include various aspects such as product quality, communication channels, response time, customer feedback, and more.

One example of a successful customer service strategy is that of Zappos, an online shoe retailer. Their strategy involves making customer service their number one priority. They invest heavily in their customer service department, including offering extensive training to their representatives. They also have a 365-day return policy, which encourages customers to shop with confidence.

As in our earlier example the Ritz-Carlton Hotel Company has a customer service strategy called "The Ritz-Carlton Gold Standards," which focuses on creating personalized experiences for guests. They use customer feedback to improve their services continually, and their employees are trained to anticipate guests' needs and exceed their expectations.

Developing a customer service strategy involves considering the needs and preferences of the target market and developing a plan that meets those needs. Here are some best practices for developing a customer service strategy:

1. Identify your target market: Understanding your customers' needs and preferences is essential to develop a customer service strategy that meets their expectations.

2. Create a customer service vision: Define your company's customer service values, goals, and objectives.

3. Train your employees: Provide your employees with the tools and training they need to deliver excellent customer service consistently.

4. Use customer feedback: Collect and analyze customer feedback to identify areas for improvement and make changes to your customer service strategy accordingly.

5. Embrace technology: Use technology to streamline customer service processes, such as chatbots and AI-powered customer service tools.

6. Empower your employees: Give your employees the authority to make decisions and resolve customer issues quickly.

By developing a customer service strategy that prioritizes customer satisfaction, businesses can improve customer loyalty and retention, drive sales, and ultimately achieve long-term success.

Here are a few reflection questions.

1. How important do you believe customer service is for a business to succeed?

2. Can you think of a time when you had a negative experience with customer service? How did it impact your perception of the business?

3. What steps could a business take to improve their customer service strategy?

4. In your opinion, what role do employees play in providing excellent customer service?

Creating a welcoming atmosphere

"Joe's Pizza" in New York City is a small, cozy pizzeria that has been around for over 40 years. The walls are decorated with photos and memorabilia from the owner's hometown in Italy, creating a warm and inviting atmosphere. The seating area is intimate, with wooden tables and chairs and soft lighting, making it perfect for a romantic dinner or a casual night out with friends.

In addition to the decor, the staff at Joe's Pizza are known for their friendly and welcoming attitude. From the moment you walk in the door, you are greeted with a smile and made to feel like part of the family. The servers take the time to get to know their regular customers and make them feel at home, while still providing top-notch service to every guest.

All these elements work together to create a welcoming atmosphere that keeps customers coming back time and time again.

Creating a welcoming atmosphere is a crucial aspect of running a successful pizzeria. When customers walk into your restaurant, they should feel a sense of warmth and comfort that makes them want to stay and enjoy their meal. The atmosphere of your pizzeria can greatly affect the overall dining experience, and therefore it should be given careful consideration.

One way to create a welcoming atmosphere is to pay attention to the decor of the restaurant. Choose colors and materials that are warm and inviting, and avoid anything that feels cold or sterile. You could incorporate cozy lighting, comfortable seating, and other design elements that make the space feel more like a home away from home.

Another key aspect of creating a welcoming atmosphere is the attitude and behavior of your staff. They should be friendly and attentive, always ready to offer assistance or answer questions. Encourage your staff to engage with customers in a positive and welcoming way, helping to make them feel at ease.

Offering complimentary snacks or drinks to customers who are waiting for a table can also create a welcoming atmosphere. This small gesture can go a long way towards making customers feel valued and appreciated.

Ultimately, creating a welcoming atmosphere is about making customers feel like they are a part of your family. It is about creating a space where people feel comfortable and relaxed, where they can enjoy good food and good company.

Here are some recommendations:

1. Use warm colors: Colors have a significant impact on the atmosphere of a place. Use warm colors such as orange, red, and yellow to create a welcoming and inviting environment.

2. Add lighting: Lighting can also affect the mood and atmosphere of a place. Use soft lighting to create a cozy and warm atmosphere.

3. Play music: Music can help set the tone and mood of your pizzeria. Choose music that complements the ambiance you want to create, whether that's calm and relaxing or upbeat and energetic.

4. Display artwork: Adding artwork to your pizzeria can make it more visually appealing and add to the welcoming atmosphere. You can display photographs, paintings, or even murals.

5. Train your staff: Your staff plays a significant role in creating a welcoming atmosphere. Make sure your staff is trained to greet customers warmly and make them feel comfortable.

6. Keep it clean: A clean and organized space creates a welcoming atmosphere. Make sure your pizzeria is always clean and tidy.

7. Offer comfortable seating: Comfortable seating can make customers feel at ease and want to stay longer. Consider offering a variety of seating options, such as booths, tables, and chairs.

Overall, creating a welcoming atmosphere is crucial for a pizzeria's success. It can make customers feel comfortable and want to return, leading to increased business and a positive reputation in the community.

1. What steps can I take to make my pizzeria more welcoming and comfortable for customers?

2. How can I better train my staff to create a warm and friendly atmosphere?

3. Have I considered all the sensory elements of my pizzeria, such as lighting, music, and scent, to enhance the customer experience?

4. How can I measure the success of my efforts to create a welcoming atmosphere and continuously improve upon it?

Handling customer complaints

Handling customer complaints is an essential aspect of providing excellent customer service. No matter how well a business performs, there will always be customers who are unhappy with something. Whether it is a mistake made by the business, an issue with a product or service, or a misunderstanding, the way in which a business handles the complaint can make or break the customer relationship.

The first step in handling customer complaints is to listen actively and empathetically. It is important to let the customer vent their frustrations and express their concerns without interruption. Show the customer that you understand their issue and that you are committed to resolving it.

Next, it is essential to take action to resolve the complaint. If possible, offer a solution or compensation to the customer. This may include providing a refund, replacement, or discount. It is important to make the customer feel valued and that their complaint is being taken seriously.

After the complaint has been resolved, it is crucial to follow up with the customer to ensure that they are satisfied with the solution. This can be done through a phone call, email, or even a handwritten note. The follow-up shows the customer that their satisfaction is a top priority and that the business cares about their experience.

In addition to resolving the complaint, it is important to learn from the experience and use the feedback to improve the business. This may involve revising policies or procedures to prevent similar complaints from happening in the future.

Overall, handling customer complaints requires patience, empathy, and a commitment to resolving the issue. By taking the time to listen to the customer, act, follow up, and learn from the experience, a business can turn a negative situation into a positive one and build a stronger relationship with the customer.

Handling negative reviews is an essential aspect of customer service, and it is crucial to handle them professionally to maintain a positive reputation for your business. Here are some steps to follow when handling negative reviews:

1. Respond promptly: It is important to respond to negative reviews as soon as possible, preferably within 24 hours. This shows that you care about your customers' feedback and are willing to address their concerns.

2. Listen and empathize: When responding to negative reviews, it is important to listen to the customer's complaint and show empathy for their situation. Acknowledge their frustration and apologize for any inconvenience caused.

3. Offer a solution: After listening to the customer's complaint, offer a solution that addresses their concerns. This could be a refund, a replacement, or any other action that would help to resolve the issue.

4. Take the conversation offline: If the issue requires further discussion, it is best to take the conversation offline. Provide the

customer with a phone number or email address where they can contact you to discuss the issue further.

5. Follow up: After resolving the issue, follow up with the customer to ensure they are satisfied with the solution provided. This shows that you value their feedback and are committed to providing excellent customer service.

By following these steps, you can effectively handle negative reviews and turn a negative experience into a positive one for your customers. Remember, how you respond to negative reviews can have a significant impact on your business's reputation, so it is essential to handle them with care and professionalism.

1. Have you ever received a negative review for your business or work? If so, how did you handle it, and what did you learn from the experience?

2. How do you respond to negative reviews online? What strategies have you found to be effective in managing your online reputation?

3. In what ways can negative reviews be an opportunity for improvement and growth in your business or work?

4. How can you use negative reviews as a learning tool to better understand your customers' needs and preferences, and to enhance your overall customer service?

Here are a few examples of good and bad ways to handle complaints.

Good example:

A customer had an issue with a product they purchased from Apple and shared their frustration on social media. Apple's customer service team quickly responded to the post, apologized for the inconvenience caused, and offered to help the customer resolve the issue. They took the conversation to a private message and provided a solution that satisfied the customer, who later thanked Apple for their prompt and helpful response.

Bad example:

A customer complained about a late delivery of their food order to a local restaurant on Yelp. The restaurant's response was defensive, blaming the delay on the customer's address being difficult to find, and dismissing the customer's concerns. The response only made the situation worse and led to other negative reviews from customers who were unhappy with the restaurant's attitude towards complaints.

Here are some reflection questions.

1. How did the company with a good example handle the customer complaint differently than the company with the bad example?

2. What impact could the good example have on the company's reputation compared to the bad example?

3. How can companies proactively avoid negative customer experiences that could lead to complaints?

4. In what ways can social media be a double-edged sword for handling customer complaints, as shown in these examples?

Chapter 8:

Online Presence

"Your online presence can make or break your business, so make sure it's worth clicking on."

In today's world, having an online presence for your business is no longer an option but a necessity. This chapter will discuss the importance of building and maintaining an online presence for your pizzeria. It will also cover the common mistakes that businesses make when building their online presence.

Many Gen X businesses are failing to keep up with the younger generation when it comes to online presence. They often view technology as a burden rather than a tool for growth. As a result, they miss out on a large portion of their potential customers who are searching for businesses online.

Having an online presence not only makes it easier for customers to find your business but also provides an opportunity to showcase your brand and connect with your customers. A strong online presence can also help build trust and credibility with potential customers.

One important aspect of building an online presence is having a user-friendly website that is easy to navigate and provides relevant information about your business. It should also be mobile-friendly since many customers search for businesses on their mobile devices.

Another critical aspect is social media presence. Having social media accounts can help increase brand awareness and engage with your customers. It's important to choose the right social media platforms for your business and consistently post relevant content.

Additionally, online reviews are crucial for building trust and credibility with potential customers. It's essential to respond to both positive and negative reviews promptly and professionally.

In summary, building and maintaining a strong online presence is vital for any business, including pizzerias. It can help increase brand awareness, connect with customers, and build trust and credibility. Failing to keep up with the younger generation in terms of online presence can result in missed opportunities for growth and customer acquisition.

Here are a few reflection questions.

1. How important do you think having a strong online presence is for a business in today's digital age?

2. Have you personally had any positive or negative experiences with a business's online presence? How did it impact your perception of the business?

3. In what ways do you think businesses can improve their online presence?

4. How do you think businesses can balance maintaining a strong online presence with the other important aspects of running a business, such as providing excellent customer service and managing day-to-day operations?

Developing a website

Developing a website is an essential aspect of building a strong online presence for any business. A website acts as the digital storefront of your business, providing a platform to showcase your products or services, engage with customers, and drive sales. In today's digital age, customers expect businesses to have an online presence, including a professional website that is easy to navigate and provides all the necessary information.

When developing a website, it is important to consider factors such as the design, functionality, content, and user experience. The website should be visually appealing, with a clear and concise layout that is easy to navigate. It should also be optimized for search engines to ensure that potential customers can find your business online.

In addition to the design and functionality, the content on the website should be informative, engaging, and provide value to the customers.

This includes information about the products or services, pricing, and any other important details. The website should also provide a way for customers to contact the business, such as a contact form or phone number.

Developing a website may seem daunting, but there are various resources available to make the process easier. Many website builders and platforms offer templates and tools to help create a professional-looking website without the need for extensive coding or design skills. Additionally, working with a web developer or designer can provide a customized and tailored approach to meet the specific needs of the business.

In summary, developing a website is crucial for establishing an online presence and engaging with customers. By creating a professional, user-friendly, and informative website, businesses can increase their visibility and reach a wider audience, ultimately leading to increased sales and growth.

One company that does a great job of developing a website is Airbnb. The website is clean, user-friendly, and visually appealing. It's easy to navigate, and the search filters are well-designed and effective.

One of the best features of the Airbnb website is the ability to search for accommodations based on specific criteria, such as price range, location, and amenities. The search results are displayed in a clear and concise manner, with high-quality images and detailed descriptions of each property.

Another great feature of the Airbnb website is the ability for hosts to create their own listings, complete with photos, descriptions, and availability calendars. This allows guests to get a detailed understanding of what they're getting before they book, which helps build trust and credibility.

In addition, the Airbnb website includes a robust review system, which allows guests to leave feedback on their stays. This not only helps future guests make informed decisions, but it also encourages hosts to maintain high standards of cleanliness and hospitality.

Overall, the Airbnb website is a great example of how to develop a website that is both user-friendly and effective at showcasing a company's products or services.

A pizzeria's website should include the following:

1. Menu: A clear and up-to-date menu that includes all available options, toppings, and prices.

2. Location and contact information: The restaurant's physical address, phone number, email address, and hours of operation should be easy to find.

3. Online ordering: A user-friendly and secure online ordering system that allows customers to place their orders for pickup or delivery.

4. About Us: A brief introduction about the pizzeria's history, values, and mission statement can give customers a sense of what the business is all about.

5. Reviews and Testimonials: Featuring customer reviews and testimonials can help build credibility and trust with potential customers.

6. Photos and Videos: Mouth-watering pictures and videos of pizzas, salads, and other menu items can make customers crave for the food even more.

7. Social Media Integration: Links to the pizzeria's social media pages (e.g., Facebook, Instagram) can encourage customers to follow and engage with the business online.

8. Specials and promotions: Highlighting current specials and promotions on the website can entice customers to order more frequently.

9. Catering and events: Information about catering services, private parties, and events can be included to generate additional business.

Overall, a pizzeria's website should be visually appealing, easy to navigate, and provide all the necessary information that customers need to order and enjoy their food.

1. How do you think a well-designed website can impact a customer's perception of your business?

2. Have you ever visited a business website that was difficult to navigate or lacked important information? How did this impact your impression of the business?

3. What steps can you take to ensure that your website is accessible to all potential customers, including those with disabilities?

4. How can you use website analytics to track customer behavior and preferences, and how can this information be used to improve your website and business overall?

Utilizing social media

Utilizing social media is an essential aspect of a business's online presence. Social media platforms, such as Facebook, Twitter, Instagram, and LinkedIn, allow businesses to engage with customers, build relationships, and establish their brand identity. Moreover, social media can help businesses reach a broader audience and increase their online visibility.

One example of a company that utilizes social media effectively is Nike. Nike has a strong social media presence across various platforms, with millions of followers. They use their social media accounts to showcase their products, promote their brand image, and share inspiring stories and content related to fitness and sports.

For pizzerias, social media can be an effective tool to build relationships with customers and promote their brand. For example, a pizzeria can use Instagram to share pictures of their pizza, showcase their menu, and feature their restaurant's ambiance. Twitter can be used to announce special deals and promotions, while Facebook can be used to engage with customers, share reviews, and promote events.

Another example of a company that uses social media effectively is Wendy's. Wendy's has become well known for their witty and sarcastic tweets, which have generated a significant amount of engagement and attention. Their social media strategy has helped them establish their brand as edgy and humorous, appealing to a younger demographic.

In summary, utilizing social media can help businesses build their brand, increase their online visibility, and engage with customers. It is essential for businesses, including pizzerias, to have a strong social media presence to remain competitive in today's digital age.

A pizzeria can do several things on social media to enhance its online presence and engage with customers, such as:

1. Post high-quality images and videos of their pizzas and other menu items, as well as behind-the-scenes glimpses of the kitchen and staff.

2. Share promotions, discounts, and special deals to encourage customers to visit the restaurant or order online.

3. Respond to customer queries and complaints in a timely and friendly manner to build trust and loyalty.

4. Share updates about the restaurant's activities, such as community events they're involved in, new menu items, or staff changes.

5. Encourage customers to share their experiences at the pizzeria on social media by using a branded hashtag and reposting user-generated content.

6. Use social media advertising to target potential customers in the local area.

Examples of pizzerias that effectively utilize social media include:

1. Domino's Pizza - The company has a strong presence on multiple social media platforms, including Facebook, Instagram, Twitter, and TikTok. They regularly post engaging content, such as

mouth-watering photos and videos of their pizzas and interactive games for customers to play.

2. Blaze Pizza - This fast-casual pizza chain has a unique and playful social media presence that appeals to a younger demographic. They frequently share user-generated content, such as photos of customers enjoying their pizzas, and run social media campaigns that encourage customers to share their Blaze Pizza experiences.

3. Pizza Hut - This global pizza chain has a dedicated social media team that responds to customer inquiries and complaints on various platforms. They also use social media to promote new menu items, launch contests, and offer discounts to customers.

By effectively utilizing social media, a pizzeria can attract new customers, retain existing ones, and strengthen its brand image.

Here are some reflection questions.

1. How can you better understand your target audience on social media and tailor your content to their interests and needs?

2. Are you actively engaging with your followers and responding to their comments and messages in a timely manner? If not, how can you improve your responsiveness?

3. How can you make your social media presence more visually appealing and consistent with your branding?

4. Are you measuring the effectiveness of your social media efforts and adjusting your strategy accordingly? If not, what metrics should you be tracking and how can you use that data to inform your decisions?

Online ordering and delivery platforms

Although we've already touched on this, it is worth bringing up again. Online ordering and delivery platforms have become increasingly important for pizzerias in recent years. They provide customers with the convenience of ordering from the comfort of their homes, and they can help pizzerias expand their customer base and increase revenue.

There are many different online ordering and delivery platforms available, each with its own set of features and benefits. Some popular options for pizzerias include:

1. Grubhub: Grubhub is a popular online ordering and delivery platform that allows customers to order from a variety of restaurants, including pizzerias. Grubhub charges a commission on each order, which can range from 5% to 30%.

2. DoorDash: DoorDash is another popular online ordering and delivery platform that allows customers to order from local restaurants, including pizzerias. DoorDash charges a commission on each order, which can range from 10% to 30%.

3. Uber Eats: Uber Eats is a food delivery platform that allows customers to order from a variety of restaurants, including pizzerias. Uber Eats charges a commission on each order, which can range from 15% to 30%.

4. Slice: Slice is an online ordering platform that is specifically designed for pizzerias. Slice charges a lower commission than other platforms, typically around 6%.

When it comes to online ordering and delivery platforms, it's important for pizzerias to choose the right platform for their business. They should consider factors such as the platform's commission rates, its user base, and its marketing capabilities. Pizzerias should also consider integrating the platform with their existing POS system to streamline the ordering process.

Overall, online ordering and delivery platforms can be a valuable tool for pizzerias looking to expand their customer base and increase revenue. By choosing the right platform and integrating it into their operations, pizzerias can provide customers with a convenient ordering experience and streamline their delivery process.

It's important to note that while online ordering and delivery platforms can be beneficial for pizzerias, they should not be relied on exclusively.

Pizzerias should also continue to offer in-person ordering and pickup options to cater to customers who prefer to order in person.

Online reputation management

Online reputation management refers to the process of monitoring, analyzing, and influencing an individual or business's online reputation. In the digital age, it is crucial for businesses to have a positive online reputation as it directly impacts their brand image and revenue.

One example of a company that excels in online reputation management is Airbnb. They have a dedicated team that constantly monitors their online presence and reviews, responding promptly and professionally to both positive and negative feedback. They also prioritize guest safety and ensure that all listings are accurately represented on their platform, which helps to maintain their positive reputation.

To effectively manage online reputation, businesses should regularly monitor online reviews and comments across all platforms, including social media, review sites, and search engine results. It is also essential to respond promptly and professionally to any negative feedback and address any issues raised by customers. By taking ownership of customer concerns and demonstrating a willingness to address them, businesses can enhance their online reputation and build a loyal customer base.

In addition, businesses should actively seek out positive reviews from satisfied customers and encourage them to share their experiences on various online platforms. This can be done through email campaigns, social media promotions, or offering incentives for leaving a review.

Overall, online reputation management is an ongoing process that requires regular monitoring and active engagement with customers. It is a vital aspect of building a successful business in the digital age.

Here are a few suggestions you use for online reputation management:

1. Monitor online reviews and comments: Regularly check social media platforms, review sites, and other online spaces where

customers may leave feedback about the pizzeria. Respond to both positive and negative comments promptly and professionally. Thank customers for positive reviews and offer solutions to any negative feedback.

2. Address negative feedback: If a customer posts a negative review or comment, it's essential to respond quickly and try to resolve the issue. Responding publicly to negative feedback shows that the pizzeria takes customer concerns seriously and is willing to make things right.

3. Encourage positive feedback: Pizzerias can encourage customers to leave positive reviews by asking for feedback after a purchase or providing incentives such as discounts or freebies. Pizzerias can also display positive reviews on their website or social media pages.

4. Stay active on social media: Pizzerias can use social media to promote their business, engage with customers, and address any questions or concerns. Regularly posting updates, pictures, and videos can keep customers engaged and help build a positive reputation.

For example, a pizzeria could hire a social media manager to monitor online reviews and comments, respond to feedback promptly, and create engaging content for social media. The pizzeria could also offer discounts or freebies for customers who leave positive reviews or refer new customers. By staying active and engaged online, the pizzeria can build a positive reputation and attract new customers.

Here are a few reflection questions.

1. How important do you think online reputation management is for businesses, especially for small businesses like pizzerias?

2. In what ways can online reputation management impact a business, positively or negatively?

3. Have you personally had any experiences with online reviews or reputation management for a business? How did the business handle it?

4. What steps can you take to improve your own online reputation management, whether for your own business or as an employee in a business?

Chapter 9:

Marketing and Advertising

"Marketing is not about selling pizza, it's about telling your pizza's story in a way that compels people to buy."

One effective way to market your pizzeria is through social media advertising. Social media platforms like Facebook, Instagram, and Twitter offer advertising options that allow you to target your ideal audience based on demographics, interests, and behaviors. You can create eye-catching ads that showcase your pizzas and other menu items, and drive traffic to your website or online ordering platform. For example, Blaze Pizza, a popular fast-casual pizza chain, uses Instagram and Facebook to promote its seasonal specials, new menu items, and giveaways. They create visually appealing ads with mouthwatering photos of their pizzas and use hashtags to increase their reach and engagement.

Another marketing strategy is to partner with other local businesses or organizations to reach new customers. For instance, you can collaborate with a nearby brewery or winery to offer a pizza and beer/wine pairing event. You can also sponsor a local sports team or school event and offer discounted pizzas to attendees. This helps you reach a wider audience and show your support for the community.

Overall, there are numerous marketing and advertising strategies that can help your pizzeria stand out in a crowded market. By leveraging various channels and partnerships, you can increase your visibility and attract more customers to your business.

Here are some examples of how a small pizzeria can effectively market and advertise their business:

1. Social media: Social media platforms like Facebook, Instagram, and Twitter are great ways to connect with potential customers and promote your pizzeria. Post mouth-watering photos of your pizzas, share information about specials or events, and engage with your followers by responding to comments and messages.

2. Local publications: Advertising in local newspapers or magazines is a great way to reach potential customers in your area. Consider creating an eye-catching ad or submitting a feature article about your pizzeria to get more exposure.

3. Community involvement: Get involved in your local community by sponsoring events or fundraisers. Offer to donate pizzas for local charity events or sponsor a little league team. This will help increase your visibility and build goodwill in your community.

4. Loyalty program: Implement a loyalty program to encourage repeat business. Offer discounts or free pizzas after a certain number of visits or give a free pizza on a customer's birthday. This will keep customers coming back and spreading the word about your pizzeria to their friends and family.

5. Email marketing: Collect email addresses from customers and send out regular newsletters with updates, specials, and exclusive offers. This is a great way to keep your customers engaged and informed about your pizzeria.

Remember, the key to effective marketing and advertising is to be creative, authentic, and consistent. Find what works best for your pizzeria and keep refining your approach over time.

Determining ROI (Return on Investment) and being strategic in marketing and advertising efforts is crucial for any small business, including a pizzeria. Here are some steps to follow:

1. Set clear and measurable goals: Before investing in any marketing or advertising efforts, determine what you hope to achieve. Do you want to increase online orders by a certain percentage? Bring in more foot traffic during specific hours? By setting clear and measurable goals, you can better determine ROI.

2. Track and measure results: It's important to track and measure the success of your marketing and advertising efforts. For example, if you run a Facebook ad campaign, track how many

clicks and conversions it generates. This will help you determine if it was a worthwhile investment.

3. Use data to inform future decisions: By tracking and measuring your results, you can use data to inform future marketing and advertising decisions. If one campaign was particularly successful, consider running a similar campaign in the future.

4. Be strategic: It's important to be strategic in your marketing and advertising efforts. Don't just throw money at any tactic that seems like it might work. Instead, carefully consider what will resonate with your target audience and invest accordingly. For example, if your target audience is primarily active on Instagram, focus your efforts there.

Example: A small pizzeria could create a marketing campaign that targets the local community, such as running ads on social media platforms or local newspapers. They could also offer special discounts or promotions to customers who refer friends and family to the restaurant. By tracking the results of these efforts and being strategic in their marketing tactics, the pizzeria can better determine ROI and make informed decisions about future marketing investments.

Creating effective marketing campaigns

Creating effective marketing campaigns for low budgets can be a challenge, but it's not impossible. With a little creativity and strategic thinking, small businesses like pizzerias can create campaigns that grab customers' attention and drive sales. Here are a few tips for creating effective marketing campaigns on a budget:

1. Define your target audience: Knowing who you are trying to reach is key to creating a successful marketing campaign. Determine who your ideal customer is and what their needs and interests are.

2. Use social media: Social media platforms like Facebook and Instagram are free and offer a great way to reach potential customers. Create engaging content that resonates with your

target audience and encourages them to share and interact with your posts.

3. Leverage email marketing: Email marketing is a cost-effective way to reach your customers and promote your pizzeria. Build an email list by offering incentives like discounts or freebies, and then create compelling emails that drive traffic to your website or encourage repeat business.

4. Collaborate with other businesses: Partnering with other local businesses can be a great way to cross-promote and reach new customers. Look for businesses that share your target audience and brainstorm ways you can work together to promote each other.

5. Offer special deals: Offering promotions and deals can help incentivize customers to try your pizzeria or come back for more. Consider offering discounts on slow nights or creating special deals for regular customers.

An example of a low-budget marketing campaign for a pizzeria could be offering a free slice of pizza to customers who follow the pizzeria's social media accounts and share a post about the offer. The pizzeria could also partner with a nearby ice cream shop and offer a discount on ice cream for customers who show their receipt from the pizzeria. These types of promotions are low-cost but can drive traffic and increase visibility for the pizzeria.

1. What are some creative and low-cost marketing ideas that could work for my pizzeria?

2. How can I tailor my marketing campaigns to reach my target audience effectively?

3. What metrics should I use to measure the success of my marketing efforts, and how can I track them?

4. What are some ways to make my marketing campaigns stand out from those of my competitors, even on a low budget?

Advertising in local media

Advertising in local media can be an effective way for a pizzeria to reach its target audience. One option to consider is using inserts instead of traditional ads. Inserts are promotional materials that are inserted into a newspaper, magazine, or other publication, and can be a cost-effective way to reach potential customers.

One benefit of using inserts is that they are often more attention-grabbing than traditional ads. People are more likely to notice an insert when flipping through a publication, as it stands out from the other pages. Inserts can also be more informative than ads, as they can include more detailed information about a pizzeria's menu, specials, and other offerings.

Another benefit of using inserts is that they can be targeted to specific geographic areas. For example, a pizzeria can work with a local newspaper to distribute inserts only to households within a certain radius of the restaurant. This can help ensure that the promotional materials are reaching the right people who are more likely to become customers.

When creating inserts or other local media advertisements, it's important to keep the messaging clear and concise. The goal should be to capture people's attention and encourage them to visit the pizzeria, so the messaging should focus on the restaurant's unique selling points and why it's worth a visit.

Overall, advertising in local media with inserts can be an effective way for a pizzeria to reach potential customers in its area. By creating attention-grabbing and informative inserts, a pizzeria can increase its visibility and attract more customers to its business.

Example: A pizzeria in a small town decides to advertise in the local weekly newspaper with inserts. They work with the newspaper to create a colorful and informative insert that includes a menu, photos of some of their popular pizzas, and a special coupon for a discount on a customer's first order. The insert is distributed to households within a five-mile radius of the restaurant. As a result of the campaign, the pizzeria sees an increase in foot traffic and online orders from new customers who mention the coupon.

Here's an example of a full-page insert for a pizzeria:

Craving a slice of heaven?

Come to Sal's Pizzeria, where we've been serving up piping hot pies for over 30 years! Our dough is made fresh daily, and we use only the highest quality ingredients to create mouth-watering flavor combinations that will keep you coming back for more.

Whether you prefer classic cheese, loaded with your favorite toppings, or one of our signature specialty pies, we've got something to satisfy every appetite. And if you're feeling extra hungry, why not try one of our delicious appetizers or a fresh, crisp salad?

But don't take our word for it – come on down and taste for yourself! With our cozy atmosphere, friendly staff, and unbeatable prices, you won't regret making Sal's Pizzeria your new favorite spot.

Don't forget – we also offer catering for all your special events, so you can enjoy the taste of Sal's no matter where you are. Call us today to place your order!

This insert includes a brief introduction to the pizzeria and its offerings, as well as a call to action encouraging readers to visit or place an order. It emphasizes the quality of the ingredients and the cozy atmosphere of the restaurant, as well as the convenience of catering for special events. The use of bold and colorful fonts and images helps to catch the reader's eye and create a sense of excitement and anticipation.

1. How can I tailor my marketing message to resonate with my local audience?

2. Am I effectively utilizing local media channels to reach my target market?

3. What incentives or promotions can I offer to entice customers to visit my pizzeria?

4. How can I track the success of my local advertising efforts and adjust my strategy accordingly?

Hosting events and promotions

Hosting events and promotions can be a great way for a pizzeria to attract new customers, engage with the community, and increase sales. There are many different types of events and promotions that a pizzeria can host, from special discounts and offers to charity fundraisers and holiday-themed events. Here are some examples of successful events and promotions that pizzerias have used to increase business:

1. Pizza Eating Contests: Many pizzerias have found success in hosting pizza eating contests, where customers compete to see who can eat the most pizza in a certain amount of time. These events can attract a lot of attention and can be great for generating buzz and publicity for the pizzeria.

2. Trivia Nights: Hosting trivia nights is another popular event that many pizzerias have used to attract new customers. By offering prizes and discounts to the winning teams, pizzerias can encourage customers to come back for future events.

3. Special Discounts: Offering special discounts or promotions, such as buy-one-get-one-free deals or half-price pizza nights, can be an effective way to attract new customers and generate repeat business.

4. Fundraisers: Hosting charity fundraisers or donating a portion of sales to a local charity can be a great way for a pizzeria to give back to the community and generate positive publicity.

One example of a successful event is the annual "Pizza Fest" hosted by Mama's Pizza in Omaha, Nebraska. The event, which takes place over a weekend in August, features live music, carnival games, and, of course, plenty of pizza. Mama's Pizza offers special discounts on pizza during the event, which attracts thousands of visitors and generates a lot of publicity for the pizzeria.

Here are some steps a pizzeria could take to plan a successful event or promotion:

1. Define the goal: The first step is to determine the goal of the event or promotion. Is it to attract new customers, reward existing ones, or generate buzz about a new menu item or promotion? Defining the goal will help the pizzeria stay focused on what it wants to achieve.

2. Choose a theme: Once the goal is defined, the pizzeria can choose a theme for the event or promotion. For example, if the goal is to attract families with children, a family-friendly theme like a "pizza-making workshop for kids" could be a good fit.

3. Set a budget: It's important to set a budget for the event or promotion to ensure that it doesn't end up costing more than it's worth. The pizzeria should consider all the costs involved, such as advertising, supplies, and staffing.

4. Plan the details: With the goal, theme, and budget in mind, the pizzeria can start planning the details of the event or promotion. This includes things like the date and time, location, menu items, activities, and marketing materials.

5. Promote the event or promotion: The pizzeria should promote the event or promotion to ensure that people know about it. This could include posting about it on social media, sending out emails to customers, and distributing flyers or other marketing materials.

6. Execute the plan: On the day of the event or promotion, the pizzeria should execute the plan and make sure everything runs smoothly. This includes staffing the event, preparing the food, and providing a great customer experience.

Example: A pizzeria could host a "Pizza and Beer Night" promotion where customers can get a free beer with the purchase of a large pizza.

The goal of this promotion could be to attract young adults who are looking for a fun and affordable night out. The pizzeria could choose a Thursday or Friday evening for the event, as those are typically busier nights for restaurants. They could set a budget of $500 for advertising and supplies, which would include printing flyers and posters, buying beer, and staffing the event. The pizzeria could plan to offer a variety of pizza toppings and craft beers to appeal to different tastes. To promote the event, they could post about it on social media, send out an email to their customer list, and distribute flyers in the local area. On the night of the event, the pizzeria could have extra staff on hand to handle the increased volume of customers, and make sure everyone has a great time.

Overall, hosting events and promotions can be a great way for a pizzeria to attract new customers, engage with the community, and increase sales. By getting creative and offering unique events and promotions, pizzerias can stand out from the competition and build a loyal customer base.

Four reflection questions about hosting events and promotions:

1. What are some unique events or promotions that could work well for my pizzeria?

2. How can I promote my events and promotions effectively to attract the most customers?

3. What are the costs associated with hosting events and promotions, and how can I ensure that they are financially feasible?

4. How can I measure the success of my events and promotions, and use that data to plan future events and promotions?

Sponsorship opportunities

Sponsorship opportunities can be a great way for pizzerias to increase brand awareness and get involved in their local communities. By sponsoring events or organizations that align with their brand values, pizzerias can increase visibility and build goodwill among potential customers.

For example, a pizzeria could sponsor a local Little League team by providing uniforms and equipment. In exchange, the team could display the pizzeria's logo on their uniforms and at their games, and the pizzeria could receive mentions on the team's social media accounts and website.

Another example of a sponsorship opportunity for a pizzeria could be to sponsor a local charity event or fundraiser. By providing food or financial support for the event, the pizzeria could gain exposure to a new audience and demonstrate their commitment to giving back to the community.

To find sponsorship opportunities, pizzerias can research local events and organizations that align with their brand values and mission. They can also reach out to local event organizers or nonprofit organizations to inquire about potential partnership opportunities.

Overall, sponsorship opportunities can be a win-win for pizzerias and the organizations they partner with, providing valuable exposure and community engagement for both parties.

1. Have you ever participated in a sponsorship opportunity as a business owner or as an individual? What did you learn from that experience?

2. How can you identify potential sponsorship opportunities that align with your brand and target audience?

3. In what ways can a sponsorship opportunity help you achieve your marketing goals and improve your brand image?

4. How can you measure the success of a sponsorship opportunity in terms of ROI and impact on brand awareness?

Chapter 10:

Financial Management

"Managing finances wisely is the foundation for a successful pizzeria."

Financial Management is an important aspect of running a successful pizzeria. It involves managing cash flow, budgeting, and forecasting to ensure the business remains profitable. Effective financial management can help a pizzeria make informed decisions, reduce financial risks, and maximize profitability.

One example of effective financial management in the pizzeria industry is the success of Pizza Hut. Pizza Hut has been successful in managing its finances by implementing a rigorous cost control program, streamlining its supply chain, and investing in technology. By doing so, Pizza Hut has been able to maximize its profitability and maintain its position as a leader in the industry.

In terms of cost control, Pizza Hut has been able to reduce its operational expenses by implementing innovative solutions such as digital ordering and delivery platforms. By investing in technology, Pizza Hut has been able to streamline its operations and reduce labor costs, while also providing customers with convenient and efficient ordering and delivery options.

In addition to cost control, Pizza Hut has also been successful in managing its supply chain. By negotiating long-term contracts with suppliers, Pizza Hut has been able to secure favorable prices for ingredients and other supplies. This has helped Pizza Hut maintain its margins and reduce its exposure to price volatility.

Overall, Pizza Hut's success in financial management can be attributed to its focus on cost control, supply chain management, and investment in technology. By effectively managing its finances, Pizza Hut has been able to maximize its profitability and maintain its position as a leader in the pizzeria industry.

Here are a few reflection questions.

1. What are some financial challenges that small pizzerias face, and how can they be overcome?

2. How can small pizzerias balance the need for growth and investment with the need to maintain profitability?

3. What are some effective strategies for managing cash flow in a pizzeria, and how can they be implemented?

4. How can small pizzerias measure their financial performance, and what metrics should they track to ensure long-term success?

Understanding financial statements

Understanding financial statements is crucial for any business, including a pizzeria, to make informed decisions and plan for the future. Financial statements provide a snapshot of a business's financial health, including its assets, liabilities, revenues, and expenses.

One of the most important financial statements for a pizzeria is the profit and loss (P&L) statement, also known as an income statement. This statement shows a pizzeria's revenues and expenses over a specific period, such as a month, quarter, or year. By analyzing the P&L statement, a pizzeria owner can see how much money the business is making, where the revenue is coming from, and where the money is being spent.

For example, a pizzeria owner might review the P&L statement for the past quarter and notice that the business had high revenues but also high expenses, resulting in a lower profit margin than expected. After reviewing the statement, the owner might decide to reduce expenses by cutting back on ingredient costs or labor expenses.

A Profit and Loss (P&L) statement, also known as an income statement, is a financial report that summarizes a company's revenues, costs, and expenses over a specified period. P&L statements provide valuable insight into a business's financial health, and it's essential for small business owners, including pizzerias, to understand how to read them. Here are some key items to look for in a P&L:

1. Revenue: This is the total amount of money the pizzeria earns from the sale of goods or services. In the case of a pizzeria, revenue could come from pizza sales, delivery fees, catering orders, etc.

2. Cost of Goods Sold (COGS): COGS is the cost of the ingredients and materials used to make the pizzas. It's important to monitor COGS to ensure that the pizzeria is pricing its products appropriately to cover costs and maintain profitability.

3. Gross Profit: Gross profit is the difference between revenue and COGS. It represents the amount of money the pizzeria has left over to cover operating expenses and generate profit.

4. Operating Expenses: These are the costs associated with running the business, such as rent, utilities, salaries, and advertising. It's essential to keep these expenses in check to ensure profitability.

Consulting an accountant can be beneficial for small business owners, including pizzeria owners, because they have the expertise to provide financial guidance and help interpret financial statements. An accountant can provide valuable insights into ways to improve profitability and optimize tax strategies. For example, they may be able to identify areas where the pizzeria can reduce expenses or suggest ways to increase revenue.

Another important financial statement is the balance sheet, which shows a pizzeria's assets, liabilities, and equity at a specific point in time. This statement can help a pizzeria owner understand the business's financial position, such as how much cash is available, how much debt is owed, and how much equity the business has.

For example, a pizzeria owner might review the balance sheet and notice that the business has a significant amount of debt owed to suppliers. After reviewing the statement, the owner might decide to negotiate payment terms with suppliers or consider refinancing the debt to reduce interest payments.

Overall, understanding financial statements is essential for a pizzeria to make informed decisions and ensure its long-term financial stability.

Reflection questions:

1. How confident do you feel in your ability to read and understand financial statements?

2. What financial statement(s) do you think are most important for a pizzeria to track and why?

3. Can you think of a time when understanding a financial statement helped you make a business decision?

4. What steps can you take to improve your financial literacy and understanding of financial statements?

Cash flow management

Cash flow management refers to the process of monitoring, analyzing, and optimizing the flow of money in and out of a business. It is essential for businesses to have a good cash flow management system to ensure that they have enough cash on hand to meet their financial obligations and make investments in the growth of the business.

One important aspect of cash flow management is monitoring the timing of cash inflows and outflows. For example, a pizzeria may have a high volume of sales on weekends, but low sales during weekdays. The pizzeria can use this information to plan its cash flow by ensuring that it has enough cash on hand to cover its expenses during the weekdays.

Another aspect of cash flow management is forecasting cash flow. This involves making projections about future cash inflows and outflows based on past performance and current trends. A pizzeria can use this information to plan for upcoming expenses and to determine when it may need to borrow money to cover cash shortfalls.

It is also important for businesses to manage their accounts receivable and accounts payable. This involves tracking the money that is owed to the business by customers and the money that the business owes to suppliers and creditors. By managing these accounts effectively, a business can ensure that it has enough cash on hand to meet its financial obligations and take advantage of opportunities for growth.

Consulting an accountant can be beneficial for pizzerias in managing their cash flow. An accountant can provide expertise in financial forecasting and help the pizzeria develop strategies for managing its cash flow effectively. The accountant can also help the pizzeria create financial reports, such as cash flow statements and balance sheets, to monitor its financial health and make informed decisions.

Overall, effective cash flow management is critical for the financial success of a pizzeria. By understanding the timing and projection of cash flows, managing accounts receivable and accounts payable, and consulting an accountant, a pizzeria can ensure that it has enough cash on hand to cover expenses and invest in growth opportunities.

A pizzeria can manage its cash flow by taking the following steps:

1. Monitor cash flow regularly: It is important to monitor cash flow regularly, ideally on a daily or weekly basis. This will allow the pizzeria to identify potential issues and take corrective action in a timely manner.

2. Forecast cash flow: The pizzeria can create a cash flow forecast to predict how much cash will be coming in and going out over a specific period. This will allow the pizzeria to anticipate any cash flow problems and plan accordingly.

3. Manage expenses: The pizzeria should keep a close eye on its expenses and look for ways to reduce them. This could include negotiating with suppliers for better prices, reducing waste, or cutting unnecessary expenses.

4. Manage inventory: The pizzeria should manage its inventory carefully to avoid overstocking or understocking. Overstocking can tie up cash, while understocking can result in lost sales.

Here are a few questions for reflection.

1. How important is cash flow management in the success of a small business?

2. What are some potential consequences of poor cash flow management?

3. What are some strategies that can be implemented to improve cash flow management?

4. How can financial software and tools be utilized to improve cash flow management?

Budgeting and forecasting

Budgeting and forecasting are essential components of financial management for any business, including a pizzeria. Budgeting involves estimating and planning for future expenses and revenue, while forecasting involves predicting future financial outcomes based on current and past data.

One effective way for a pizzeria to create a budget is to use historical financial data to determine average revenue and expenses over a certain period of time. For example, a pizzeria might look at its revenue and expenses over the past year to create a budget for the upcoming year.

Forecasting can be more challenging, as it requires predicting future financial outcomes based on a variety of factors, such as market trends and competition. However, forecasting can also be critical to ensuring that a pizzeria is prepared for future financial challenges and opportunities.

For example, a pizzeria might forecast the impact of opening a new location or offering a new menu item, and adjust their budget accordingly. This can help them avoid financial difficulties and take advantage of growth opportunities.

In addition to helping a pizzeria manage its finances more effectively, budgeting and forecasting can also be useful for securing financing from banks or investors. When a pizzeria can demonstrate that they have a solid plan for managing their finances and achieving growth, it can make them more attractive to potential lenders or investors.

Overall, effective budgeting and forecasting are critical components of financial management for a pizzeria and can help ensure long-term success.

An example of a company that does a great job with budgeting and forecasting is Starbucks. The coffee giant regularly reviews its financial performance and forecasts future sales based on a variety of factors, such as consumer trends and store traffic.

This allows them to adjust their budget and make strategic decisions to improve profitability and drive growth. Additionally, they provide regular updates to investors and stakeholders on their financial performance and outlook, which helps build trust and confidence in the company's financial management.

To create a budget and forecast, a pizzeria should first establish their financial goals and objectives. This will help them identify how much money they need to make and where they need to focus their resources. Then, they can follow these steps:

1. Estimate their revenue: This involves estimating how much money the pizzeria will make from sales.

2. Determine their costs: This includes fixed costs like rent and salaries, as well as variable costs like ingredients and utilities.

3. Calculate their profit or loss: This is the difference between revenue and costs.

4. Use historical data: A pizzeria can use their financial statements from previous years as a guide for budgeting and forecasting.

5. Adjust for changes: They should consider any changes in the market, competition, or consumer preferences that could affect revenue and costs.

6. Review regularly: They should monitor their budget and forecast regularly and adjust as necessary to ensure they are on track to meet their financial goals.

An example of budgeting and forecasting for a pizzeria could be:

The pizzeria wants to increase their revenue by 10% over the next year. They estimate their revenue for the year will be $500,000. They calculate their fixed costs to be $200,000 and their variable costs to be $250,000, leaving them with a projected profit of $50,000. They then review their budget and forecast quarterly and make adjustments as necessary to ensure they are on track to meet their financial goals.

By budgeting and forecasting, the pizzeria can ensure they are making the most of their resources and have a plan for achieving their financial objectives.

Here are a few reflection questions.

1. How can budgeting and forecasting help a small business like a pizzeria to stay financially stable in the long term?

2. What are some common mistakes that small business owners make when it comes to budgeting and forecasting, and how can they be avoided?

3. How can a pizzeria ensure that its budgeting and forecasting process is accurate and reliable?

4. How can a pizzeria adjust its budget and forecast in response to unexpected changes or challenges, such as changes in the market or a global pandemic?

Cost control strategies

Cost control strategies are important for any business, including a pizzeria, to maintain profitability and financial stability. These strategies involve identifying and reducing unnecessary expenses while maintaining the quality of products and services.

One example of a cost control strategy for a pizzeria is to regularly review and adjust menu prices based on the cost of ingredients and other expenses. For instance, if the cost of cheese and other toppings increases, the pizzeria may need to adjust the price of pizzas to maintain a consistent profit margin.

Another cost control strategy is to minimize waste and optimize inventory management. For example, a pizzeria can reduce waste by carefully measuring ingredients, properly storing leftover ingredients, and using them in other menu items. They can also optimize inventory by tracking inventory levels and ordering only what is needed to avoid overstocking and waste.

Additionally, using energy-efficient equipment and reducing energy consumption can also help a pizzeria reduce costs. This can include using LED lighting, energy-efficient ovens, and properly maintaining equipment to ensure it is running efficiently.

One successful example of a pizzeria that has implemented effective cost control strategies is MOD Pizza. The company has been able to keep their prices competitive while maintaining high-quality ingredients and customer service. They achieve this through efficient inventory management, minimizing waste, and reducing energy consumption using energy-efficient equipment and LED lighting. They also have a comprehensive training program for their staff to ensure they are properly trained on cost control strategies.

Overall, cost control strategies are essential for a pizzeria to maintain financial stability and profitability while still providing high-quality products and services to their customers.

There are several ways a pizzeria can implement cost control strategies to manage their expenses and increase their profits. Here are some examples:

1. Regularly review expenses: One of the simplest ways to control costs is to regularly review and track expenses. This will help identify areas where costs can be reduced, such as renegotiating supplier contracts, reducing waste, or cutting down on unnecessary expenses.

2. Optimize inventory management: Effective inventory management can help reduce waste and save money. Pizzerias can use software tools to track inventory levels, set reorder points, and forecast demand, which can help prevent overstocking or stockouts.

3. Reduce labor costs: Labor costs can be a significant expense for pizzerias. One way to control labor costs is to optimize employee schedules to ensure that staffing levels are appropriate for the business demand. Pizzerias can also consider cross-training employees to perform multiple tasks, which can help reduce the need for additional labor.

4. Implement energy-saving measures: Pizzerias can reduce their energy costs by implementing energy-saving measures such as using energy-efficient appliances, turning off equipment when not in use, and adjusting temperature controls.

5. Negotiate better pricing: Pizzerias can negotiate with suppliers for better pricing and discounts, especially for bulk purchases.

An example of cost control strategies implemented by a pizzeria is as follows:

ABC Pizzeria regularly reviews their expenses and tracks them using accounting software. They noticed that they were spending too much on supplies, such as napkins, straws, and paper cups. To address this, they renegotiated their supplier contracts and switched to a different supplier that offered a better price. They also implemented inventory management software, which helped them track their inventory levels and reorder points. As a result, they reduced their waste and avoided overstocking. Finally, they optimized their employee schedules and cross-trained their employees, who helped them reduce their labor costs.

A few questions for reflection.

1. How can a small business like a pizzeria balance the need for cost control with the desire to maintain high-quality products and services?

2. What are some potential consequences of not implementing effective cost control strategies in a pizzeria?

3. How can regular monitoring of expenses help a pizzeria identify areas where cost control strategies can be implemented?

4. In what ways can cost control strategies evolve and change over time to adapt to a pizzeria's evolving financial situation?

Chapter 11:

Sustainability and Community Engagement

"Small steps towards sustainability and community engagement can lead to big impacts for a pizzeria."

Patagonia, a California-based outdoor clothing and gear company, is renowned for its unwavering dedication to sustainability and community engagement. Since its inception, Patagonia has championed environmental protection and encouraged sustainable practices throughout its operations.

The company's sustainable practices are evident in its use of only organic cotton in its clothing, investment in renewable energy, and a recycling program for its products. Patagonia's commitment to sustainability extends beyond its own operations, with the company advocating for environmental protection and sustainable practices globally.

In addition to sustainability, Patagonia places a significant emphasis on community engagement. The company supports local environmental organizations and encourages its employees to volunteer in their communities. The company's platform called "The New Localism" is a prime example of their commitment to sustainability and responsible business practices in local communities.

"The New Localism" promotes sustainable and responsible business practices in communities, which encourages other businesses to prioritize sustainability and community engagement. This approach has helped Patagonia to build a loyal customer base, and the company's success has inspired other companies to follow in their footsteps.

Overall, Patagonia has proven that it is possible to prioritize sustainability and community engagement while still achieving business success. The company's efforts serve as an excellent example for other businesses to follow in creating a more sustainable future.

Incorporating sustainable practices

Incorporating sustainable practices into a business model is becoming increasingly important as consumers are becoming more aware of the impact of their purchasing decisions on the environment. Sustainable practices not only benefit the environment but can also lead to cost savings and enhance a company's reputation.

There are several ways that a pizzeria can incorporate sustainable practices into their business. One way is to source ingredients locally to reduce transportation emissions and support local farmers. Another way is to use eco-friendly packaging and utensils made from materials like paper or compostable plastic instead of traditional plastic.

Pizzerias can also consider implementing energy-saving measures such as installing LED lighting, using energy-efficient appliances, and reducing water usage. By taking steps to conserve resources, pizzerias can not only reduce their environmental impact but also save on utility costs.

In addition, pizzerias can educate their customers about their sustainable practices and encourage them to make sustainable choices. For example, providing recycling bins and offering incentives for customers who bring in their own reusable containers.

An example of a pizzeria that incorporates sustainable practices is Pizza Fusion. The company uses organic and locally sourced ingredients in their pizzas, as well as eco-friendly packaging and utensils. They also have a recycling program and use energy-efficient appliances in their stores. Pizza Fusion has not only gained a reputation for their delicious pizzas but also for their commitment to sustainability.

Incorporating sustainable practices in a pizzeria can provide several benefits for both the business and the environment. Here are a few reasons why a pizzeria should consider implementing sustainable practices:

1. Cost savings: Sustainable practices such as energy-efficient lighting and water-saving devices can reduce utility bills, saving the pizzeria money in the long run.

2. Enhanced brand reputation: Customers today are increasingly concerned about environmental issues, and they prefer to do business with companies that share their values. By adopting sustainable practices, a pizzeria can enhance its brand reputation and attract eco-conscious customers.

3. Improved employee morale: Employees are more likely to be engaged and motivated when they work for a company that aligns with their values. By incorporating sustainable practices, a pizzeria can improve employee morale and retain talent.

4. Environmental benefits: Sustainable practices can have a positive impact on the environment by reducing waste, conserving natural resources, and minimizing the carbon footprint of the business.

Overall, incorporating sustainable practices in a pizzeria can help the business save money, attract customers, improve employee morale, and contribute to a healthier planet.

Research suggests that millennials and Gen Z customers are particularly concerned with sustainability and environmental responsibility. These younger generations prioritize companies that demonstrate a commitment to social and environmental causes and are more likely to support businesses that align with their values.

As they continue to age and become a larger share of the consumer market, it becomes increasingly important for businesses to incorporate sustainable practices to attract and retain these customers.

Here are some reflections questions.

1. What are some sustainable practices that can be incorporated into the pizzeria's operations?

2. How can the pizzeria effectively communicate their commitment to sustainability to customers?

3. In what ways can the pizzeria engage with the local community to promote sustainability?

4. What are some potential challenges and obstacles the pizzeria may face when incorporating sustainable practices, and how can they be overcome?

Community outreach and engagement

TOMS was founded in 2006 with a mission to provide shoes to children in need. For every pair of shoes purchased, TOMS donates a pair to a child in need. Over the years, TOMS has expanded its giving to include eyewear, clean water, safe births, and bullying prevention programs.

TOMS' commitment to giving back has also extended to community outreach and engagement. The company has launched various programs to engage with communities and support local causes. One such program is the TOMS Local Giving Program, which provides funding to organizations that address issues such as homelessness, education, and youth development in the communities where TOMS employees live and work.

In addition to the Local Giving Program, TOMS has also launched the TOMS Animal Initiative, which supports animal welfare organizations, and the TOMS Climate Action Fund, which invests in renewable energy projects. Furthermore, TOMS has taken steps to reduce its environmental impact by using sustainable materials in its products and reducing its carbon footprint.

To effectively communicate its commitment to community outreach and engagement, TOMS has created a dedicated section on its website that showcases its giving programs and impact. TOMS also uses social media to highlight its community engagement efforts and encourage its followers to get involved.

In summary, TOMS Shoes has demonstrated a strong commitment to community outreach and engagement by launching various giving programs and initiatives, supporting local causes, and reducing its environmental impact. The company effectively communicates its efforts to customers through its website and social media channels, inspiring others to get involved and make a difference in their own communities.

There are many ways a pizzeria can engage in community outreach beyond sustainability initiatives. Here are some examples:

1. Participating in local events: The pizzeria can participate in local events such as fairs, festivals, and community gatherings. This will give them an opportunity to meet and connect with members of the community.

2. Supporting local schools and sports teams: The pizzeria can support local schools and sports teams by sponsoring events, donating food for fundraisers, or offering discounts to students and athletes.

3. Hosting fundraising events: The pizzeria can host fundraising events for local charities or organizations. They can donate a portion of their sales to the cause or host a special event with all proceeds going to the charity.

4. Donating to local causes: The pizzeria can donate food or funds to local causes such as food banks, homeless shelters, and other organizations that support the community.

5. Partnering with other local businesses: The pizzeria can partner with other local businesses to cross-promote each other and offer joint discounts or promotions to customers.

Overall, community outreach is a great way for a pizzeria to connect with the local community, build relationships, and increase brand awareness.

1. In what ways do you believe community outreach can benefit a small business like a pizzeria?

2. What are some creative ways a pizzeria can engage with the local community beyond traditional marketing and advertising?

3. How can a pizzeria measure the success of their community outreach efforts?

4. What are some potential challenges a pizzeria may face when engaging in community outreach, and how can they be overcome?

Supporting local causes

Supporting local causes is a great way for a business to give back to the community and build a positive reputation. Many companies choose to support causes and charities that align with their values and mission, and this can be a great way to demonstrate their commitment to social responsibility.

One company that is known for its support of local causes is Ben & Jerry's, the Vermont-based ice cream company. Ben & Jerry's has a long history of social activism and environmental advocacy, and they have made supporting local causes a key part of their business model. The company has a dedicated team that works on social and environmental issues, and they partner with local organizations to support a range of causes, from food justice to climate action.

One example of Ben & Jerry's community outreach efforts is their "Scoop Shop of the Month" program. Each month, the company highlights a different Scoop Shop location and donates a portion of their sales to a local nonprofit organization chosen by the shop's staff. This program not only supports local causes, but it also helps to build relationships between the company and its customers.

Another example of Ben & Jerry's community outreach is their "Stamp Stampede" campaign. This campaign encourages customers to stamp messages about money in support of campaign finance reform, and the company donates a portion of the proceeds from their Stamp Stampede merchandise to support organizations working on this issue.

Incorporating similar community outreach efforts can be beneficial for pizzerias looking to build strong ties with their local community. For example, a pizzeria could partner with a local food bank or homeless shelter to donate pizzas or hold a fundraiser to support their cause. They could also host a "giveback night" where a percentage of their sales go to a local nonprofit organization, or sponsor a local sports team or event to build brand recognition and support community engagement.

Effective communication is key in community outreach efforts. A pizzeria can effectively communicate their support of local causes through social media, email newsletters, and in-store signage. They can also engage with customers and the community by attending local events and networking with other local businesses.

It's important to note that supporting local causes may also come with challenges and potential obstacles.

While supporting local causes can be a great way for businesses to give back to their communities, it can also come with some challenges and potential obstacles. Some of these challenges include:

1. Choosing the right causes: With so many worthy causes in a local community, it can be challenging for a business to decide which ones to support. The business must determine which causes align with their values and mission while also considering the impact they can make.

2. Managing expectations: Once a business decides to support a local cause, they must manage the expectations of the organization they are supporting, as well as their employees and customers. This can include setting clear boundaries on what kind of support the business can provide and communicating expectations around timelines and outcomes.

3. Balancing community needs with business needs: While supporting local causes can be a great way to give back to the community, businesses must also ensure that their support doesn't compromise their bottom line. This can be especially challenging for small businesses with limited resources.

4. Avoiding controversy: Some causes or organizations may be controversial or polarizing, and businesses must be careful to avoid alienating customers or creating negative publicity. It's important for businesses to thoroughly research the

organizations they are supporting and consider any potential backlash.

Overall, supporting local causes can be a rewarding and impactful way for businesses to engage with their communities, but it's important to approach it thoughtfully and carefully to avoid potential challenges and obstacles.

1. How can supporting local causes benefit a business and its community?

2. What are some effective strategies for identifying and selecting local causes to support?

3. How can a business measure the impact of its support for local causes?

4. What are some potential challenges and obstacles that a business may face when supporting local causes, and how can they be overcome?

Building goodwill in the community

Starbucks, the coffee giant has implemented various initiatives to give back to the communities in which it operates.

One example of this is the Starbucks Community Service Program, which encourages employees to volunteer in their local communities. Starbucks also supports local nonprofit organizations through its Starbucks Foundation, which has donated millions of dollars to organizations focused on education, environment, and community development.

In addition, Starbucks has made efforts to be an environmentally responsible company. The company has committed to sourcing 100% of its coffee and palm oil from ethical and sustainable sources and has implemented recycling and waste reduction programs in its stores.

Through these initiatives, Starbucks has built a positive reputation and strong relationship with its customers and communities. This has resulted in increased customer loyalty and support, as well as a positive impact on the local communities where Starbucks operates.

A pizzeria can build goodwill in the community by engaging in various activities that benefit the local community. One way to do this is by sponsoring local events such as school carnivals or sports tournaments. By doing so, the pizzeria can gain visibility among the local community and promote their business while supporting the community.

Another way to build goodwill in the community is by offering discounts or promotions to residents, such as a discount for first responders or teachers. This shows that the pizzeria values and supports the local community and its members.

The pizzeria could also partner with local charities or non-profit organizations and donate a portion of their sales to support their cause. This not only helps to build goodwill in the community but also provides support for important local causes.

Lastly, the pizzeria could host events such as fundraisers or community nights where a portion of the sales go towards a local cause or organization. This not only provides an opportunity for the community to come together and support a good cause, but also promotes the pizzeria as a business that cares about the community.

Brother's Pizza in Crawfordsville, Indiana for instance, every year during the holidays hosts an event on their street. They call is Christmas on Green Street. They bring in reindeer, a slay, Santa and Mrs. Claus, then invite the community out. They give away a thousand toys to the children who show up. During this event people can be seen wrapped around the building, waiting to get into the restaurant.

Overall, building goodwill in the community requires the pizzeria to have a genuine interest in supporting and giving back to the local community. By doing so, the pizzeria can establish a positive reputation and become a valued member of the community.

1. What are some benefits of building goodwill in the local community for a small business like a pizzeria?

2. How can a pizzeria identify the needs and wants of their local community to effectively build goodwill?

3. What are some creative ways a pizzeria can engage with the local community to build goodwill?

4. In what ways can building goodwill in the community help a pizzeria differentiate itself from competitors and attract new customers?

Chapter 12:

Conclusion

"Building a successful and sustainable pizzeria is like crafting the perfect pizza - it requires a balance of key ingredients, careful planning, and a commitment to quality at every step."

We have explored various aspects of running a successful pizzeria. Some key takeaways include:

1. Quality ingredients and attention to detail are crucial for making delicious pizza that will keep customers coming back.

2. It is important to have a strong online presence, including a user-friendly website and active social media accounts, to attract new customers and engage with existing ones.

3. Effective marketing strategies, such as hosting events and promotions, offering sponsorship opportunities, and incorporating sustainable practices, can help increase brand awareness and customer loyalty.

4. Financial management is essential for long-term success, and understanding financial statements, cash flow management, budgeting and forecasting, and cost control strategies can all contribute to a profitable business.

5. Community engagement and building goodwill are important for fostering positive relationships with customers and supporting local causes.

Overall, running a successful pizzeria requires a combination of delicious pizza, effective marketing and financial management strategies, and a commitment to sustainability and community engagement. By prioritizing these areas, pizzeria owners can create a thriving business that is beloved by its customers and contributes to the local community.

Now that you've completed the workbook and gained a wealth of knowledge and strategies to improve your pizzeria, it's time to put them into action. It's important to remember that implementing these strategies will not happen overnight, and it may require significant effort and resources. However, the benefits of investing in your pizzeria's financial management, sustainability, community engagement, and more can be substantial and long-lasting.

To encourage implementation, start by prioritizing which strategies will have the most significant impact on your pizzeria's success and sustainability. Break down these strategies into smaller, achievable steps that can be executed over time. Consider enlisting the help of your team to ensure that everyone is on board and invested in making these changes.

Continuously monitor and evaluate the effectiveness of these strategies to ensure that they are aligned with your pizzeria's goals and mission. Adjust as needed and celebrate successes along the way.

Remember, incorporating sustainable practices, engaging with the community, and prioritizing financial management can not only improve your pizzeria's bottom line but can also make a positive impact on the environment and the world around you. By acting and implementing the strategies learned in this workbook, you can create a more successful, sustainable, and socially responsible pizzeria.

1. What did you learn about incorporating sustainable practices in a business?

2. What did you learn about the importance of community engagement and outreach in business?

3. What strategies did you learn about for cost control and budgeting in business?

4. What did you learn about financial management and understanding financial statements in business?

Final Thoughts

Running a successful pizzeria is not an easy feat, but with the right strategies, it is definitely achievable. Throughout this workbook, we have covered various aspects of running a pizzeria, including financial management, marketing, customer service, sustainability, and community engagement. By implementing the strategies outlined in each chapter, a pizzeria owner can set themselves up for success.

As a final thought, it is essential to remember that running a successful pizzeria requires dedication, hard work, and a commitment to continuous improvement. It is crucial to regularly assess your operations, gather feedback from customers and employees, and adjust your strategies accordingly. With each adjustment, you can move closer to your goal of running a thriving pizzeria.

So, my call to action is simple: take the knowledge and strategies you have gained from this workbook and implement them in your pizzeria. Don't be afraid to try new things and take risks to improve your operations. Always keep the customer at the forefront of your decision-making and strive to create an exceptional experience for them. With a focus on continuous improvement, dedication, and hard work, you can run a successful and thriving pizzeria. Good luck!

Here are some resources that may be helpful for those looking for further information on running a successful pizzeria:

1. National Restaurant Association - This association provides resources and information for restaurant owners, including information on best practices and industry trends.

2. Pizza Today - This publication offers news, trends, and expert advice for pizza industry professionals.

3. International Pizza Expo - This annual trade show features educational sessions, workshops, and networking opportunities for pizzeria owners and operators.

4. SCORE - This nonprofit organization offers free business advice and mentoring services for entrepreneurs.

5. Small Business Administration - The SBA offers a variety of resources and support for small business owners, including access to funding, educational resources, and mentoring services.

6. Local business organizations - Many cities and towns have local business organizations that provide support and resources for small business owners. These organizations may offer networking opportunities, educational events, and other resources.

7. Industry associations - There are several industry associations for pizza professionals, including the Association of Independent Pizzerias and the North American Pizza and Culinary Academy. These organizations offer resources, networking opportunities, and educational events for their members.

By utilizing these resources and seeking out additional support and guidance, pizzeria owners can continue to learn and grow as they work to build and sustain a successful business.

Notes:

Notes:

www.ingramcontent.com/pod-product-compliance
Lightning Source LLC
Chambersburg PA
CBHW080836220526
45467CB00008B/2295